DEDICATION

For H. H. Richardson in love and veneration,

For my Mother and Brother in love and memory,

For Arthur in love and hope,

For the City in love and celebration.

-- *James D. Van Trump*

In 1884, the County of Allegheny chose the designs of Henry Hobson Richardson for its new County Buildings. The third Court House and the accompanying Jail as built differ in important ways from the buildings as they appear here. The surroundings are fictitious, but convey the small-scale, heavily-industrial city of Pittsburgh where the Court House rose.

MAJESTY OF THE LAW

THE COURT HOUSES OF ALLEGHENY COUNTY

James D. Van Trump

Pittsburgh History & Landmarks Foundation

Published by
Pittsburgh History & Landmarks Foundation
450 The Landmarks Building, One Station Square
Pittsburgh, PA 15219

Manufactured in the United States of America

Additional material and captions by Walter C. Kidney
Edited by Walter C. Kidney and Louise King Ferguson

Library of Congress Catalog Card Number: 88-61708
ISBN 0-916670-12-0

ILLUSTRATION SOURCES

Allegheny County Department of Works: 16
County of Allegheny: 25, 51 (both), 52 (top), 53, 55, 56, 60, 65, 73 (top), 76 (both)
Archives of Industrial Society, University of Pittsburgh Libraries: 52 (bottom)
Joseph M. Barr, Jr.: 168
Buffalo and Erie County Historical Society: 33
Carnegie Library of Pittsburgh: 4, 71, 73 (bottom), 91, 96, 98, 99, 100 (both), 101, 102 (bottom), 103 (both), 133, 141 (bottom), 143 (bottom), 151
Clyde Hare: Jacket, 39, 155, 170, 171
Houghton Library, Harvard University by permission: 45, 172
Ohio Historical Society: 5
William H. Pierson: ii, 58, 61, 66, 80, 82 (both), 108, 111, 112, 113 (bottom), 115 (top), 129, 147 (right), 149 (bottom right), 157
Pittsburgh History & Landmarks Foundation: v, vi, viii, x, 2, 10, 13, 18, 21, 22, 24, 26, 27, 30, 38 (both), 41 (both), 42, 43 (both), 44, 47 (both), 48, 55, 64, 84, 87, 89, 90, 95, 102 (top), 105 (both), 106 (both), 109, 110, 113 (left), 115 (bottom), 126, 131, 132, 140, 141 (top), 142, 143 (left), 144, 147 (left), 149 (left and bottom left), 153, 165
UDA Architects: 169 (Carol Highsmith, photographer)
University Archives, University of Pittsburgh: 31

CONTRIBUTORS

The Pittsburgh History & Landmarks Foundation gratefully acknowledges the generosity of the following contributors to the writing and publication of this book.

Bicentennial Commission of Allegheny County
James W. Knox, Chairman

The 1988 Bicentennial Committee of the
Court of Common Pleas of Allegheny County

The Edgar Kaufmann Charitable Foundation

Kirkpatrick & Lockhart

The Lawyers' Fund Committee of the
Allegheny County Bar Association

Members of the
Allegheny County Bar Association

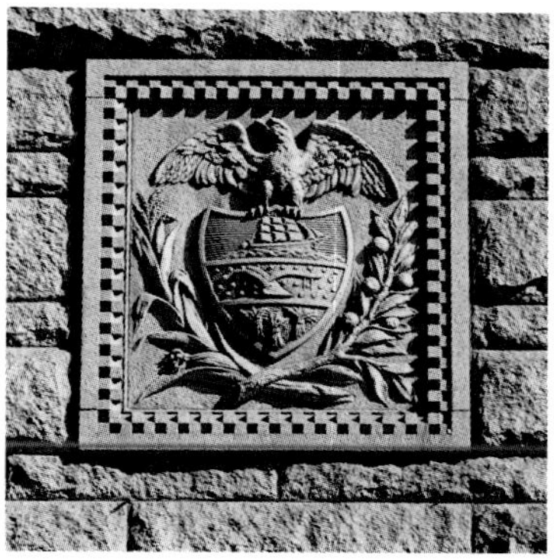

This book was released on September 24, 1988 by the Pittsburgh History & Landmarks Foundation and the Bicentennial Commission of Allegheny County in honor of the celebration of the completion of the Allegheny County Court House and Jail and the bicentennial celebrations of Allegheny County and the Court of Common Pleas.

Detail, Ross Street entrance of the Court House.

CONTENTS

Foreword:
Of Love and Court Houses viii

The Pride of the West:
Pittsburgh's First Court House 1

Grant's Hill, Paradise:
An Interlude 11

Solon's Dome:
The Second Court House 17

Grant's Hill, and a Fire:
An Interlude 27

The Phoenix Tower:
The Story of Its Building, 1882-83 31

The Phoenix Tower:
The Story of Its Building,
January-June 1884 49

The Phoenix Tower:
The Story of Its Building
July-December 1884, and 1885 67

The Phoenix Tower:
The Story of Its Building, 1886-87 77

The Phoenix Tower:
The Story of Its Building, 1888 85

The Tower Dedicated:
An Interlude 92

The Tower Achieved:
The Court House and Jail in 1888 97

The Tower and the City:
1889-1913 127

The Tower and the City:
1914-70 145

The Tower and the City:
Since 1970 161

Epilogue 173

Bibliography 175

Index 177

FOREWORD

OF LOVE AND COURT HOUSES

During most of the course of my life, I have approached downtown Pittsburgh from the east, along Fifth Avenue. At the top of a certain rise of ground the street falls away toward the city's center and there, sharp and clear even against the skyscrapers, has always stood Richardson's great Court House and its magnificent tower.

It has been a part of my life for so long that I'm not quite sure when I first got the idea of writing about it; but being a writer, I did at some point begin to write and speak about the Court House, and about the Jail as well. When I was in charge of recording the structures for the Historic American Buildings Survey, the idea crystallized further.

In due course this book was begun, but even after the research was started I became more and more intrigued with the idea of expanding the original scope to include all the court houses that have existed in Pittsburgh. It would be interesting to see how these various structures reflected the state of the city as it grew and changed: thus, there would have to be some examination not only of the buildings but also of their surroundings.

I also wanted to establish a record of how these structures were created and how they existed afterward. All possible sources have been combed for such information, and the research has been long and arduous. The record is not complete; it rarely ever is. Some documents are gone beyond recovery. (We will never know, for instance, how many primary documents disappeared in the great Court House fire of 1882; few exist from before this time.) The documentation of Richardson's Court House is extensive and fairly complete.

Although I am an architectural historian, and aware that Richardson's Court House is a scholar's "plum," I have particularly resisted the temptation to become overly *kunsthistorisch*. With regard to architecture, I have said or quoted what seemed to be necessary for the basic story. Other architectural historians pursuing their own goals are free to erect their own shining palaces on the record established here; to establish that record is the prime purpose of this book.

Richardson's Court House and Jail are great works of art; but as such they belong to the whole body of humanity, not just to scholars. A work of art is both a reflection and a transformation of our total humanity; in the highest sense it is a gesture of affirmation, an act of love.

The works of love are known, and I believe that what was said or written by most of those who had anything to do with the building of Richardson's Court House and Jail is evidence that something more than genius was at work. I confess, also, that I cannot regard these buildings with dispassion. I have known them all my life. They contain much that I feel about art and humanity, and in them is symbolized the love that I bear for my native city—Pittsburgh.

This book is therefore a labor of love. Possibly the eye of love is sometimes faulty, but if that be so, then it is part of the record. Conscious of my task, I have tried to make that record whole and true.

James D. Van Trump

View of the City of Pittsburgh in 1817: *lithograph based on a sketch by Mrs. E. F. Gibson. The Courthouse spire appears to the left of the Pittsburgh Point, dominating what is still little more than a village. A flatboat and a keelboat represent the city's commerce, while in the right background an industrial chimney suggests its future.*

THE PRIDE OF THE WEST

PITTSBURGH'S FIRST COURT HOUSE

The recovery of Pittsburgh's first public building of any importance is no small feat, and the result at best a mutable and clouded triumph. The vanishment of provincial grandeurs is proverbial; minor buildings are as little remembered as lesser heroes. This being so, the search among old records is surely a pious act. A voyage among an infinity of dead local buildings to find the form, the essence, the use of a structure once the pride and the symbol of an emerging city, undertakes a resurrection profitable to the present.

How is one to find an image of the first Pittsburgh Court House that will present it in its brightest, clearest aspect and yet suggest its place in the youthful city? One has long had in mind a favorite picture that seems to be eminently suitable for this purpose—a watercolor sketch made by a Mrs. E. F. Gibson on her wedding journey to the West in 1817. Here the little town sits quietly and equally with the land. There seems to be a freshness, a clearness in the water and the air. All's new, all's bright. There is not yet too much smoke; the skyscraper of the town is the Court House.

Let us, in the eye of the mind, station ourselves at her viewpoint and then move over the pale water toward the city. We will land at the Monongahela Wharf where the keel boats and log rafts bound for the West are tied. We will walk past the street where houses and taverns alternate with "yards" where hollyhocks and marigolds bloom. Market Street is now the most important street in Pittsburgh and it leads directly into the Diamond where the Court House raises its cupola and its spire. But before we look more closely at the building we must enquire into the means by which it came there.

After the final conquest of Western Pennsylvania by the British forces in 1758, counties were formed for administrative and judicial purposes. The Province of Virginia also laid claim to the land around Pittsburgh, calling it the District of West Augusta. The dispute was settled in 1780 and the present Southwestern Pennsylvania boundaries surveyed by 1785. In the beginning of settlement these areas were often quite large, but they were later subdivided into smaller counties as need arose. By an act of the Pennsylvania Legislature of September 24, 1788, Allegheny County was formed from territory that had formerly been embraced in Westmoreland (established in 1773) and Washington (1781) Counties, and other areas north of the Ohio and west of the Allegheny Rivers within the limits of Pennsylvania. By act of the General Assembly of March 12, 1803, Allegheny County was reduced to its present dimensions. Pittsburgh was, in the last years of the eighteenth century, the legal and judicial center of a considerable territory.

Under the 1788 act organizing the County of Allegheny, trustees were appointed to select lots in a reserve tract, afterwards laid out as the town of Allegheny, across the Allegheny River from Pittsburgh. Within this area it was directed that a court house be built. Since there was more territory than population on that side of the river, this provision caused great dissatisfaction in Pittsburgh. As a consequence, a legislative act was secured in 1791 that directed that the County building for courts and other business be erected in Pittsburgh.

After the question of the location of the county seat had been settled, and pending the erection of suitable buildings, courts were held in existing buildings, beginning in December 1788. In 1800 the courts were moved into the newly-completed Court House.

A tract of land constituting a kind of public square had already been established in the emerging city near the Point. George Woods and Thomas Vickroy, in laying out the new town of Pittsburgh for the Penn family in 1784, continued and augmented the gridiron military plan

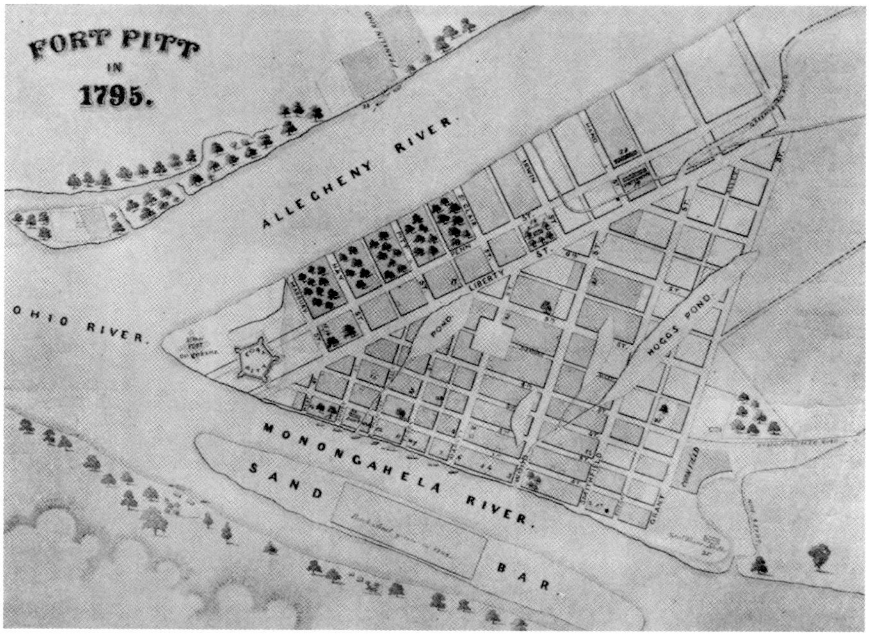

Pittsburgh in 1795, as shown in a map of the 1870s. In fact, no vestiges of Fort Duquesne and very few vestiges of Fort Pitt remained at this time, and the street grid north of Liberty Street went—on paper, at least—all the way to the Point. The Diamond lies to the east of the westernmost pond. The abrupt rise of Grant's Hill, the Hump lowered so many times in later years, begins to the east of Hogg's Pond.

created by Colonel John Campbell in 1764. In these new streets, adjacent to the original Campbell layout, the Diamond (the future Market Square) was located. Although the lots of the Penns' plan were for sale, the public tract was a gift from the proprietors to the new town that as yet had no real corporate existence.

These public squares, or "diamonds," were common in early Pennsylvania towns. One writer on early Pittsburgh says, "They were intended as practical provisions for the overnight parking of coaches, wagons, and horses rather than for beautification. They were and still are social centers for the towns." The Scotch-Irish, who played a predominant role in the development of Pittsburgh, brought with them the name given to the square. One historian observes that the "use of the term 'diamond' for 'square' in Pennsylvania. . .knits the ties with Ulster. Outside Pennsylvania and Ulster the only occurence of 'diamond' of which I am aware is on the original plot of Cleveland, Ohio."

The chief use of the Diamond was as a site for the first Allegheny County Court House. Until 1841, when the Greek Revival Court House of John Chislett was completed on Grant's Hill, this small square brick building, with its slender Georgian cupola and spire, was the fountain of legal life in the frontier town as well as the social hub of the area. At the turn of the century the city was still very small, and most of its business could be conducted within sound of the Court House bell.

The Court House, which occupied the western half of the Diamond, was completed in two sections. The two lateral one-story wings that contained offices for the Sheriff, Register, Recorder, and other County offices were probably finished in 1796; but the square central structure where the courts were held was barely completed when the court proceedings began to be held there in 1800. The belfry lacked the bell, some of the upper rooms were yet unplastered, and the space before the building was only then being paved.

We can summon some idea of the Court House by consulting the rather meager graphic evidence from the past, as well as a few published descriptions. The structure survived until 1852, into the early days of photography, but so far as is known no photograph of it has survived. There are apparently no graphic representations of the interior of the building. Other than pictures, our chief sources are literary—descriptions from the books of early nineteenth-century travelers, local reminiscences, articles in periodicals, and occasional newspaper notices. Even this material is not exactly abundant; the descriptions are haphazard and unsystematic; dates often vary.

Despite all difficulties—we cannot reconstruct the stairs—we can form a general idea of this little Court House, the pride of the West. It is square, built of brick, two-storied with a hipped roof, from the center of which rises a square louvred belfry and above that a slim spire. There is a paucity of cornice, but there is a belt course between the first and second floors.

The first Court House, in a painting of 1894 by John D. Tucker that is based on earlier sketches. The building is shown in its later years, its wings gone and replaced by market sheds. The Diamond was to contain a succession of market buildings until 1961.

The sashed windows are multi-paned, and above them are flat brick arches in the Georgian style of the Eastern Seaboard. In the center of the main facade on Market Street is a door flanked by two fluted wooden columns that support a rather subdued triangular pediment, the latter reported as ''slightly ornamented.''

It appears also that

> *there were wings to the right and left of the main edifice, one story high, each having two rooms with entrances from the street. The several county offices were in these wings, the Treasurer and Commissioners occupied those toward the south and the Register and Recorder (offices combined into one) and the Sheriff had those toward the north.*

These wings were gabled and on a line with the brick sidewalk in front of them. The main building was about 70 feet square and was about 45 feet high, not including the spire. The wings were about 15 feet high.

Lacking any extant visual evidence, we must depend entirely on written records for our description of the interior. The main courtroom occupied the ground floor and was paved with large, square bricks, like those for the pavement outside. Supporting the floor above were six or eight fluted wooden pillars about two feet in diameter, having Corinthian (or some say Doric) capitals and resting upon square-paneled pedestals. "These were severely gashed, having been found convenient by loafers for testing their penknives." Georgian architectural amenities were not universally appreciated or respected in the West.

The judges' bench and the jury box were in the rear of the courtroom, facing the entrance. The judges' bench seated the president judge and four lay associate judges; it was elevated above the floor and was reached by steps at the northern end. The jury box was on one side of the bench, and the prisoner's box on the other. The space within the bar used by the attorneys was separated from the rest of the room by a fence. On either side of the courtroom were lobbies for spectators, jurors, and witnesses. A modern account states also that "for the convenience of spectators there was a gallery around all four sides of the hall. The entrances to the grand and petit jury rooms were from this gallery." One is inclined to place credence in this statement, because of a row of windows that appear between the first and second stories in the side elevation of the Court House shown in a sketch and a painting. Although we lack any precise description of the interior or even the crudest sketch plan, it is difficult to see how the balcony could have been fitted in. It appears that the Recorder's Court was located on the second floor and that the Grand Jury room was on the same floor. Here again we have no precise idea what the exact functions of the individual rooms were, nor their dimensions.

Almost as mysterious as the details of the plan is the dating of the building. We do not know exactly when it was begun. One unconfirmed account states that the wings were finished in 1796, and the main building in 1799; but this is contradicted by another saying that "in 1800 the main building was barely completed, some of the upper rooms being yet unplastered, although the county offices had been removed to the wings two years before." We do know that in 1801 a bell was placed in the Court House steeple and the town bellman rang it before each session of court and to announce fires. The courts were installed in the Court House by the turn of the century and continued to sit there until 1841.

The third State House at Columbus, Ohio, 1816.

What was the architectural ancestry of the first Court House? Its basic composition, a four-square mass with a hipped roof and central belfry and spire, stemmed from the New England meeting house, medieval in origin but further developed by English colonists in the seventeenth century. Its style was adapted later for schools and town halls, and came into use for court houses and capitols, as witness the third Ohio State Capitol at Columbus, Ohio, in use from 1816 to 1852. But Pittsburgh was not noted for any large contingent of New Englanders in the late eighteenth century, although undoubtedly there were some. The style of both the exterior and interior, judging from the rather limited graphic evidence and the literary descriptions, seems in the end to favor the Georgian of

Philadelphia. Certainly there was nothing medieval about the interior arrangement of the building, although the multiplicity of use, so notable a facet of its history, might argue a medieval precedent.

The Court House was used for every purpose for which the citizens could lawfully assemble. The Diamond was the center of early Pittsburgh, and the new Court House partook liberally of this centrality. Since it was also the only considerable building in town, it was the hub of citizen activity, and was used for occasions of great public importance. The memorial service for General George Washington was held in the newly-completed buildings on January 8, 1800. A town meeting was held in the Court House on August 26, 1812 to organize the defense of Pittsburgh in the War of 1812. Religious congregations, which as yet had no permanent buildings of their own, sometimes held services there. The Court House rooms echoed to the gossip of loafers and housewives as well as to the eloquence of many of the legal lights of the Pittsburgh bar, James Ross, William Wilkins, and Walter Forward.

The Court House was sometimes the Borough Hall. From the incorporation of the Borough in 1794 "there was no fixed meeting place for the council of the borough, which met at the Court House, the market house or one of the taverns, chiefly the latter." The taverns probably won out over the Court House because of their liquid refreshment. After the turn of the century, however, water was available. In 1802, for a better water supply, a well paid for by the County was dug at the Court House. (Even in those early days, though, there was a question as to how clear and pure the water may have been; probably whiskey at the tavern would have been safer for the Borough Council—though not conducive to the most decorous ordering of public affairs.)

Perhaps the most interesting facet of the chequered career of the first Court House was its use as a community playhouse. Fortescue Cuming, a traveler who spent the winter of 1807-08 in Pittsburgh, says of the Court House theatre: "The jury room upstairs is sometimes converted into a very good temporary theater where private theatricals are practiced in the winter by the young gentlemen of the town." Later he says, "There are also two dramatick [sic] societies in Pittsburgh, one composed of the students of the law and the other of respectable mechanics. They occasionally unite with each other in order to cast the pieces to be performed with more effect."

The Court House in its rightful role lent color to town life. Ceremonies in connection with the early courts of Allegheny County had a certain drama and pageantry, and the bench and bar at that early period, although few in number, were mighty in point of ability.

Henry Marie Brackenridge relates:

> *When our judges of Nisi Prius and Oyer and Terminer came once a year on their circuit they were received with no little show and*

> *parade.*
>
> *As is still the custom in England, the venerable sages of the law were met by the principal gentry and lawyers marshaled by the High Sheriff not in coaches, for we had none, but on horseback for it was then the only mode of traveling. On the bench our Judges did not wear gowns or put on wigs. I have been informed, however, that Justices McKean and Bryan at the first Court of Oyer and Terminer held in Pittsburgh sat in scarlet robes!*
>
> *But compared to the plain manners of our present citizen judges, there was no little pride, pomp and circumstance attending their movements. Their honors were carefully rigged out in suits of black and cocked hats; they went to and from Court preceded by the High Sheriff bearing a long white wand before them—and what had a still more imposing effect on the boys and populace, something of a martial character was imparted to their procession by its being preceded by the rattling of a drum. Dennis Loughy, the blind poet, generally officiated at these occasions at a respectable distance before the dignitaries beating his rr-ran-rr-ran-tan decked in an old uniform coat, the red lapels taken off, and barefooted, not so much for the want of means to purchase a pair of shoes,* as for the convenience of feeling his way with his toes.

It must have been a brave sight to see the little procession moving along Market Street, the staid justices led by a barefooted blind poet beating a drum. Let it not be said that the streets of early Pittsburgh lacked for interest.

The County courts and the United States district courts for the Western District of Pennsylvania were held in the first Court House from 1800 until 1841, when they were moved to the new building on Grant's Hill.

Concomitant to any court house is the inevitable jail: there must be some place to house prisoners awaiting trial. When Pittsburgh was part of Westmoreland County the jail as well as the court house were in Hannastown; but after the creation of Allegheny County a log house situated near the corner of Fourth and Market Streets was used to hold prisoners. When the structure became undesirable, the County purchased in 1793 a lot situated on an alley now called Delray Street, about 140 feet west of the West Diamond and running parallel to it. On the western side of this alley, a short distance south of what is now Forbes Avenue, the new two-story stone County Jail was completed, whether about the same time as the Court House or, more probably, in 1817. The building was surrounded by a stone wall; the entire lot was enclosed by a high board fence. In the center of the Jail's facade was a door, "studded with nail-heads as large as copper cents." A flight of stone steps led up to this medieval-looking door, and to complete the prison-like aspect of the place, the windows were secured by iron bars. Save for these ominous adjuncts the building resembled an ordinary Scotch-Irish stone dwelling house—albeit one in which no one really cared to stay even for a short time. This structure was used until the jail on Grant's Hill was completed in 1841.

But let us return to the fabric of the Court House. For some it was the wonder of the age in the western world. However, in time, there *were* dissenting voices. An account of 1826 contains a satirical and unflattering description:

> *As for lofty glittering spires and cupolas no such necessary objects to direct the way-faring man and embellish the city withal are to be seen among us. The only ambitious structure that aspires to any height within the corporation is the steeple of the county court in which is suspended a most musical bell that threatens to bring down the daring fabric now tottering to its fall with every sound of its cracked and crazy voice. This solitary spire standing like a scathed pine in the center of a large clearing around which the smoke from heaps of burning brush continually hovers is no more palpable to the optics of the coming traveler at a reasonable distance than the houses which enclose the little space of the Public Square, alias the Diamond.*
>
> *Not a single public square is visible within the corporate limits save and except the contracted dirty spot of ground just mentioned. . . . On election occasions, indeed from twilight until midnight, the vacant part of it is held in undisputed possession by a crowd of clamorous boys and overgrown children who alarm the vicinage by shoutings and the display of burning balls and blazing tar barrels to the great terror of all well-disposed persons and without having before their eyes the fear of the city authorities, who, for the time being, are divested of all manner of authority.*

Contempt for the Court House grew. The multiplicity of use created wear and tear on the fabric; time added to the depredations of the penknives of the loafers. In the 1830s the *Advocate* spoke of "the old rookery of a Court House which is a disgrace to the city," but by that time construction on the Doric temple of justice on Grant's Hill had begun.

The old building was sold at auction in 1841 for $575 to William Eichbaum; the land on which it stood could not be sold because of restrictions in the Penn deed. The aging structure was not, however, torn down immediately; it served as a market house until it was demolished in 1852 to make way for the new Diamond Market House. (The old bell of the Court House, with its "cracked and crazy voice," had already been salvaged and placed on the new jail on Grant's Hill.)

The first Court House as seen in its last days, between 1841 and 1852, was commemorated in a painting by John D. Tucker in 1894. He based his painting on a sketch by T. P. Robitser that appeared in the *Pittsburgh Directory* in 1859, which in turn was based on a sketch by an unknown artist of an earlier day. Since both the painting and the Robitser sketch show that Court House stripped of its two side wings, we assume that the drawing was made after the two side wings had been demolished and after the erection of the market stalls.

We have come as close as we can to the spired building in the green town seen in Mrs. Gibson's water color; but there is much that remains unclear. In our view, after the judges and the drummer have disappeared through the Corinthian pillars, we are left with a blankness of brick and wood. We cannot enter. What, we can only repeat again, was it *really* like? What did the young men say in the upper room when they were play acting? But we can not even reach the upper room. Where, *where* were the stairs?

O dolor, to always be questioning the past! And to receive so small an answer! But suddenly we remember the drummer gone before the judges and we are rebuked. A stillness falls in the historical air. The blind poet must have found the stairs with his naked toes. Are our imaginations less sentient, any less sure?

Pittsburgh in 1790, already surveyed as a town but still no more than a village of scattered houses, most of them of logs. The Point is to the left; to the right are the twin eminences of the Bluff by the river and the Hill behind, their height exaggerated here. Grant's Hill rises between them.

GRANT'S HILL, PARADISE

AN INTERLUDE

The level land behind the Point at Pittsburgh is a flat alluvial plain. Beyond it, the hills for which Pittsburgh is so famous begin to rise. The first of these is called Grant's Hill. *The Franklin Magazine Almanac* of 1820 describes Grant's Hill:

It is about sixty feet high, rather regular and not steep except on the western side. A great part of it is suffered to remain in lawn; and if it were found in any other kind of scene, it would be a charming spot—it would be highly romantic on the shore of a lake or bordered by an ancient wood or crowned with a ruin or mouldering cottages. This interesting little hill which would have been a fairy rendezvous in the olden time was named after Major James Grant.

Grant was a Scottish officer on the staff of General John Forbes, commander of the successful British expedition in 1758 against the French and Indians at Fort Duquesne. On the night of September 13, 1758, at about eleven o'clock, Grant led the forward detachment to the hill top. The next morning Grant decided to attack Fort Duquesne. He probably hoped to clothe himself with glory by presenting General Forbes, on his arrival, with a *fait accompli* in the form of a captured fort. But just as British General Edward Braddock had done in 1755, Grant chose to use European military tactics against the French and Indians. Instead of advancing by stealth on the fort, he ordered reveille sounded in the morning; this not only aroused the French and Indians but allowed them to attack Grant's small force before it had made much progress beyond the hill. The result was disaster. By November, however, General John Forbes and his troops successfully reached Fort Duquesne, and the town of Pittsburgh was born.

Of all the early literary descriptions of Grant's Hill, the best is written by Hugh Henry Brackenridge (1748-1816), a lawyer and writer who came to Pittsburgh in 1781. Brackenridge was a tireless promoter of cultural activities in the frontier town. He was responsible for printing the first newspaper west of the Alleghenies: the first issue of the *Gazette* appeared on July 29, 1786. For this issue Judge Brackenridge described the youthful city and Grant's Hill:

> *To the eastward is Grant's Hill, a beautiful rising ground discovering marks of ancient cultivation, the forest having long ago withdrawn and shown the head and brow beset with green and flowers. From this hill two chrystal fountains issue, which in the heat of summer continue with a limpid current to refresh the taste. It is pleasant to celebrate a festival on the summit of this ground. In the year 1781, a bower had been erected covered with green shrubs. The sons and daughters of the day, assembling joined the festivity viewing the river at a distance and listening to the music of the military on the plain beneath them. When the moonlight rising from the east had softened into grey, the prospect, a lofty pile of wood enflamed with pyramidal risings, illumined both the rivers and the town which far around reflected brightness. Approaching in the appearance of a river god, a swain begirt with weeds natural to these streams and crowned with leaves of the sugar tree, hailed us and gave prophetic hints of the grandeur of our future empire. His words I cannot remember, but it seemed to me for a moment that the mystic agencies of deities well known to Greece and Rome were not a fable, but that the powers unseen haunt the woods and rivers, who take part in the affairs of mortals and are pleased with the celebrance of events that spring from great achievement and from virtue.*

Brackenridge was also a poet, and this description of a rustic fete, with its bower and its swain in the guise of a river god, so reminiscent of Renaissance entertainments, has poetic charm and power.

After writing of Grant's defeat, Brackenridge continues to note that "bones and weapons are yet found on the Hill, the bones white with the weather, the weapons covered with rust." And having spoken of recent bones, he goes on to describe an ancient Indian burial mound:

> *On the summit of the hill is a mound of earth supposed to be the catacombs or ancient burying ground of the savages. There can be no doubt of this, as on opening some of the tumuli or hills of earth, bones are found. In places where stones are plenty, these mounds are raised of stone and skeletons are found in them.*

The Grant's Hill mound still existed in 1817, since it was mentioned by John Palmer, a British traveler: "This hill is also remarkable for an Indian tumuli in the garden of Mr. Ross which he obligingly permitted us to view. It is in the form of a truncated cone, thirty feet in diameter by ten feet high."

Henry Marie Brackenridge (1786-1871), the son of Hugh Henry, published his *Recollections of Persons and Places in the West* in 1868. Remembering the Grant's Hill of his youth he writes:

The hill was the favorite promenade in the fine weather, and on Sunday afternoon. It was pleasing to see the line of well-dressed ladies and gentlemen, and children, nearly the whole population repairing to this beautiful green eminence. It was considered so essential to the comfort and recreation of the inhabitants, that they could scarcely imagine how a town could exist without its Grant's Hill! There was a fine spring halfway up, which was supposed to afford better water than that of the pumps, and some persons even thought it was possessed of medicinal properties—which might be the case, after a pleasant afternoon's walk, and the toil in overcoming the steep ascent.

Pittsburgh in 1840, from Grant's Hill. *The buildings to the far left background appear to be the Jail and the main body of the nearly-completed second Court House. The outline of the first Court House appears in the distance, left of the picture's center. In the center middle ground the Pennsylvania Canal crosses on its way to the tunnel through Grant's Hill.*

Perhaps Grant's Hill was chiefly known as the location of John Marie's tavern. Since the general area was one to which the townspeople resorted for pleasure, a place of refreshment was almost a *sine qua non*. However, Marie's place was not just a pleasure pavilion, but a real inn where travelers could be accommodated; for many years it was Pittsburgh's leading tavern. Its enclosure contained more than six acres and was called, after its location, "Grant's Hill." The tavern itself was located just outside the borough limits. The grounds, traversed by graveled walks, were kept in a nice state of cultivation with shrubberies and flower gardens. The present Court House, the City-County Building, and a small part of the County Office Building now occupy the larger portion of the site of the former domain of John Marie.

But ''paradise on the Hill'' could not remain, because the city was growing outward into the hills beyond the river plains of the Triangle. By the early nineteenth century, Pittsburgh had already encircled Grant's Hill. The new municipality of Pittsburgh and Allegheny County had begun to look toward larger horizons; the Diamond—flat as it was—had come to look rather meager. Why not look to the hills—and especially to one of no great altitude which would ''command'' the city slightly and sufficiently but not too much? Grant's Hill, if it *was* a little steep on the western side, was just the right height for a subtle and yet majestic architectural dominance by the law. Pittsburgh was eager to have a new Court House, and in 1834 James Ross sold part of the Grant's Hill plot to the Allegheny County Commissioners to accommodate the new Court House and Jail.

We must return once more to Henry Marie Brackenridge's account of Grant's Hill. He thus laments the disappearance of the hill's early amenities:

> *What a change in the appearance of Pittsburgh . . . since the time when I used to roll over and over on the smooth velvet side of Grant's Hill!*
>
> Sed fugit interea, fugit irrevocabile tempus. *Yes, that beautiful hill itself which might have enjoyed a green old age has been prematurely cut to pieces and murdered by barbarous hands! The shallow pond at its base where we used to make our first attempts at skating has been wickedly and willfully filled up, and is now concealed by brick buildings; the croaking of the town frogs having given place to men more noisey still than they. What is passing strange, as if by mockery of nature, the top of the hill is half-covered by an enormous reservoir of water thrown up there by means of steam engines, while the remainder is occupied by a noble cathedral church. What is still more lamentable the hill itself has been perforated, and a stream has been compelled to flow through the passage, at an expense that would have discouraged a Roman emperor. Streets have been cut in its sides, as if there were a great scarcity of ground in this new world; and in time, houses will rise up along them like those of the Cowgate in Edinburgh, thirteen stories on one side and half a story on the other.*

Although this phenomenon happened elsewhere in Pittsburgh, it did not occur on Grant's Hill. As Leland Baldwin says;

> *Brackenridge's prophecy of a Pittsburgh Cowgate might well have come true had not the city fathers . . . seen fit to cut off layers from*

the top of the hill. The first cut on "the hump" was probably made before 1837 [possibly to accommodate the entrances to the new Court House]; *it left the Roman Catholic cathedral and water reservoir perched far above the street. Additional cuts were made in 1844 and 1847, and the final one was begun in 1911. Altogether the hill was cut down in some places as much as sixty feet.*

We shall deal with these slicings and cuttings in more detail as we come upon them in our narrative.

As we look now from the lower level of the town, in about 1830, Grant's Hill glimmers and wavers before us like a dream. In that dream, figures and objects are moving into the picture—drays and horses and men with pickaxes and spades. They address themselves to "paradise" and their object is ruin, or perhaps we should politely call it change. It is no use, we say to ourselves, the dream of paradise always disappears, vanishes; we share Henry Marie Brackenridge's lament because all the original wonder of Grant's Hill is being destroyed. More philosophically, though, we must consider that this *will* happen, and that a new vision of municipal glory will be vouchsafed to us.

Now once more, as we look intently at the vanishing greenness, the youthful swain as seen by the elder Brackenridge again appears, girt with river weeds and crowned with the leaves of the sugar tree. He is saying something about manifest destiny: prophecies possibly of empire. All we can see behind him as he speaks are pale sandstone walls and Doric columns, and above them Solon's dome, the next stage of our journey in time.

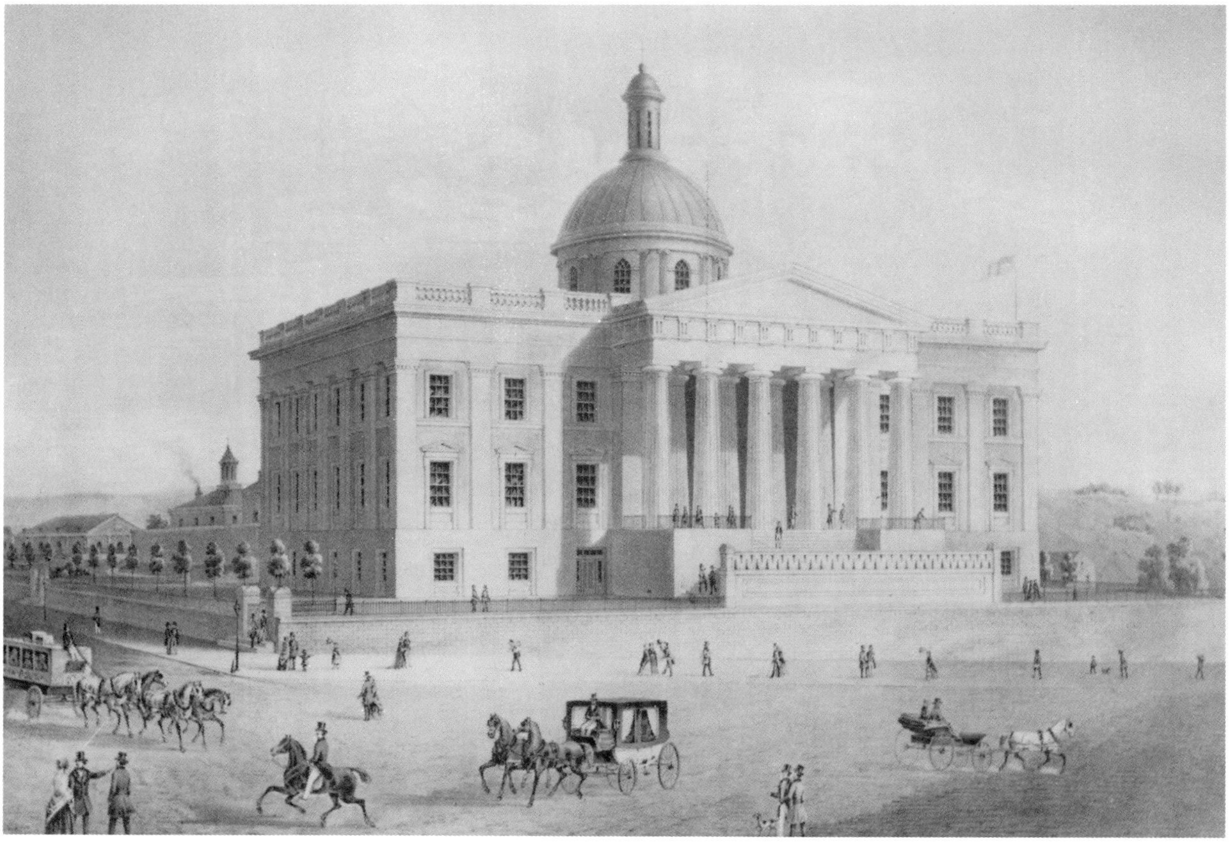

The second Court House around 1850, with its jail to the immediate left. The Hump had already been cut down somewhat, so that the building stands on a low terrace above the street. The architectural compromise of Greek and Renaissance motifs is well shown.

SOLON'S DOME

THE SECOND COURT HOUSE

The image of local law and justice was uplifted to a memorable degree after 1830 by the construction of the second Allegheny County Court House on Grant's Hill. Above the towers and spires, and the smoking chimneys of the lower town, appeared its Doric portico and its expansive dome. There are many contemporary views of the structure, mostly engravings and lithographs. Several views drawn from the Ohio River below the Point or from Mount Washington show how the new "temple of justice" dominated the city. By 1850 Pittsburgh's reputation as the Smoky City was already well established, and the view of the classical facade—the columns and the dome through veils of smoke—must have been extremely dramatic and impressive. Athens has come again, although in something of a new guise, and Solon is happily remembered.

John Chislett, who designed the new Court House, was the chief architect of Pittsburgh in the 1830s and a respected, well-known gentleman. His life and career have never been studied fully and there is still much information that we do not have about him, including a reasonably complete list of his buildings; the major accomplishments of his career can be established fairly well. Chislett was born in 1800 in England. He served his apprenticeship at Bath with an architect, a Mr. Harris. It is not known when Chislett came to America, but by 1833 he was living in Pittsburgh. In that year he joined the Third Presbyterian Church, whose handsome spired Ionic building, erected in 1834, he probably designed though we have no exact documentary proof. He also used the Ionic order in his severe porticoed design for the Bank of Pittsburgh, erected in 1834. The next year Chislett designed the first office building in the city, Burke's Building on Fourth Avenue.

Miraculously this building is still extant; it is the only Greek Revival building left in downtown Pittsburgh. Chislett must have designed several other buildings in the same style for the rapidly growing metropolis, but again documentary evidence is not available. He was busy with the Court House from 1836 to 1841, but in 1844 he was made superintendent, architect, and landscape designer of the Allegheny Cemetery; he held this position until his death in 1869. The cemetery, located in Lawrenceville on the Allegheny River above Pittsburgh, was one of the first of the great Romantic suburban cemeteries of the nineteenth century. Chislett designed the charming Tudor gate on Butler Street (1848) and a pinnacled Gothic receiving vault; the former is still extant. These Gothic elements testify to the increasing eclecticism of nineteenth-century architectural practice, but the canon of Chislett's known work is largely Greek.

In the 1830s and '40s, Pittsburgh was almost completely a Greek Revival city. Greek Revival represented the last important phase of the Renaissance, and also was one of the earliest and most pervasive of the nineteenth-century revivals. This was especially true in youthful America; the Revival provided the new frontier cities and towns of the expanding nation with their first monumental architecture. During its relatively brief ascendancy on the American frontier, between 1830 and 1850, it contributed to the developing image of the Midwestern cities of the United States.

Greek Revival architecture was solid and rational, anchored splendidly in the Classical past at a time when that past carried a bit more weight than it does now. It was also bright, poetic, infused with the glow of youth, an ephebic architecture for ephebic appreciation. The Greek Revival—houses (great and small), schools, warehouses, hotels, churches—all austere, all simply designed, presented Pittsburgh's Grecian

John Chislett's Butler Street Gateway to Allegheny Cemetery (1848), with the 1868 Administration Building by Barr & Moser to the left. Victorian architecture dressed for the occasion, and Chislett abandoned his usual Classicism to produce a handsome Tudor gateway of warm gray sandstone, appropriate as the entrance to a solemn place that had as well the character of a Romantically landscaped park.

mask, and also its youthful face, to the world. The forges roared and the factories smoked; but the Classical facade, while it lasted, was grand with columns. The city was never again to be so homogeneous or so fair in architectural style. The Greek Revival in Pittsburgh has always seemed to me to be the physical presentment of a very beguiling image of the City of Man. This Greek nobility of mien in some ways masked the development of the new industrialism, the emerging technology of which Pittsburgh was to be one of the foremost exponents; but the Classical tradition was still strong enough to make it also the *very* face of the city.

And so we come to the second Court House, Solon's dome, the masterpiece of John Chislett, the very Greekness of a Greekly-Revived Pittsburgh. Why Solon? I remember in my childhood meeting a retired lawyer, who remembered from *his* youth the Greek Court House on the hill. He referred to it as Solon's temple. Solon was one of the archons of Athens, a demi-god, a hero in the grand antique mould. He was a reformer who tried to adjust inequities between the rich and the poor, a promulgator and a giver of laws that were carved on wooden prisms long preserved in Athens. He was a poet. It was he who, near the end of his life, resisted the tyrant Pisistratus, whose lover he had once been. Solon was one of the Seven Sages of Antiquity, whose wisdom and wonder has become legend.

And Solon, against the majestic Doric columns of the Pittsburgh Court House, seemed real to me. The Court House, presided over by the great fluted deities of stone, seemed an eternal platform, dedicated to drama. Solon could move there as well as the lawyers of the 1840s.

But beyond memories and legend we do know certain historical facts. The second Court House was designed in 1834 or 1835. It also is probable that construction was begun early in 1836, because the cornerstone was laid on October 13, 1835. Construction proceeded at a leisurely pace, for the building was not occupied until June 25, 1841, when the first courts were held. This chronology, although not perfect, at least establishes the dating with some certitude and corrects the chronologies of some previous histories.

The Court House was rectangular, of yellow-gray sandstone, 165 feet long by 100 feet deep. The building consisted of two stories on a high basement, although it was sometimes referred to as a three-storied structure. It was crowned by a circular domed cupola 37 feet in diameter over a central rotunda 60 feet in diameter and 80 feet high, bearing a lantern. The height of the building from ground line to the tip of the lantern was 148 feet. All elevations of the structure above the podium were characterized by the use of the colossal Doric order with each bay articulated by pilasters, the whole topped by a severely treated, rather heavy, entablature and a balustrade. The windows of the main floor of the front elevation were capped by triangular pediments. In the center of the main facade was a massive hexastyle Doric portico with fluted columns, each six feet in diameter at the base. Behind the first row of pillars was another of four shafts flanked on either side by pilastered piers. Above was an unornamented triangular pediment. Since the base floor was considerably high, the portico was reached by a tall flight of steps. The building sat on an elevated terrace facing Grant Street, approached by further flights of steps rising from Fifth Avenue and Diamond Street (now Forbes Avenue).

The changing level of Grant Street necessitated the high sandstone wall along the street. An engraving of the building, published in 1843, shows the terrace wall as being rather low, but further reductions in the street level tended to ''sky'' the Court House, making it difficult to see it properly from the street. The building was most majestic from a distance. Seen through mists of smoke as in a luminous twilight it was not too difficult to think of ancient Greece and the Athenian Acropolis.

The basic form of the building was not Greek, however. The elevations featuring the colossal order on a podium, crowned above with an entablature and balustrade, had been a standard Renaissance device from the sixteenth century, as were the pedimented windows. The central portico of the main facade was also nothing new, but in this case the heavy, brooding Doric quality of the porch gave it an air of advancing almost violently from the center of a Renaissance palace facade. What in the end ''contains'' and in a sense subdues the portico is Chislett's firm control of the over-all Greek austerity.

In plan the central part of the building was Roman, a variation of the Pantheon theme since it was essentially a porticoed rotunda to which wings had been attached on either side. To architectural purists, the use of the dome with the Greek temple form has always been troubling. Why should Solon in the nineteenth century have a dome, when in his own day he never knew one? ''Why not?'' replied the Greek Revivalist, as many an American court house and capitol building before 1860 can testify. A growing eclecticism of form as well as style made light of such incongruities.

The interior of the building was as impressive as the exterior. As far as is known, no views of the inner space survive. Thanks to *Fahnestock's Pittsburgh Directory* for 1850 we do have floor plans of the three main stories, with some dimensions from various sources and descriptions of the rotunda. The Doric portico led into the great circular space which was the center of the *piano nobile* or main courtroom floor. The rotunda, paved with flagstone, was 60 feet in diameter and 50 feet high to the base of the dome. It was ringed by eight Corinthian columns, again in a colossal order. The ceiling of the dome, considered ''exceedingly beautiful,'' was executed with stucco work with enriched paneling. Leading from the rotunda on the same floor were four courtrooms, those of the U.S. Circuit Court, the Supreme Court, the Courts of Oyer and Terminer (Common

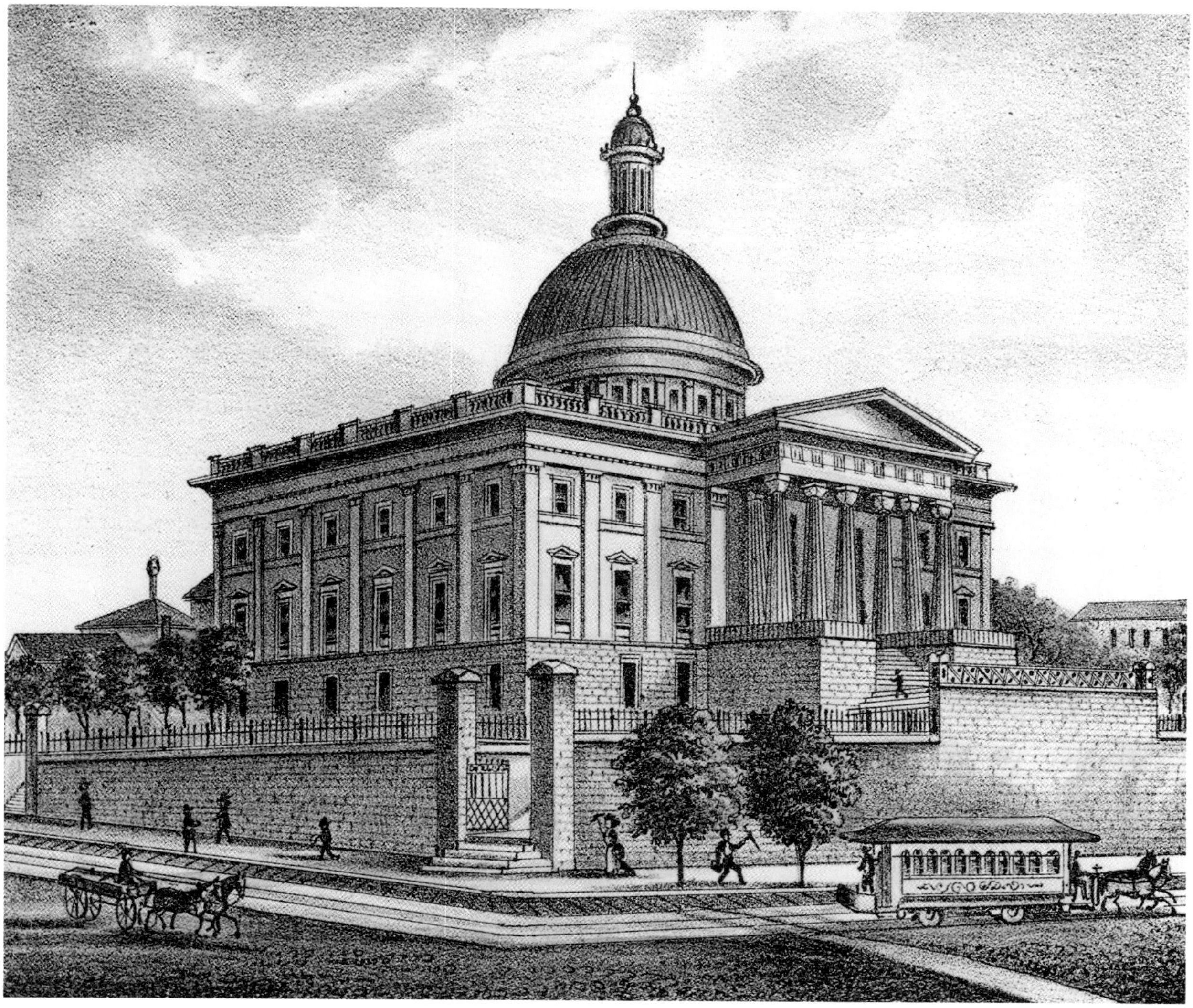

The second Court House in the Mid-Victorian period. The lithograph is crude—the horsecar on Grant Street could hardly have turned the corner at a right angle—but the increasing height above street level after two further Hump cuts is apparent.

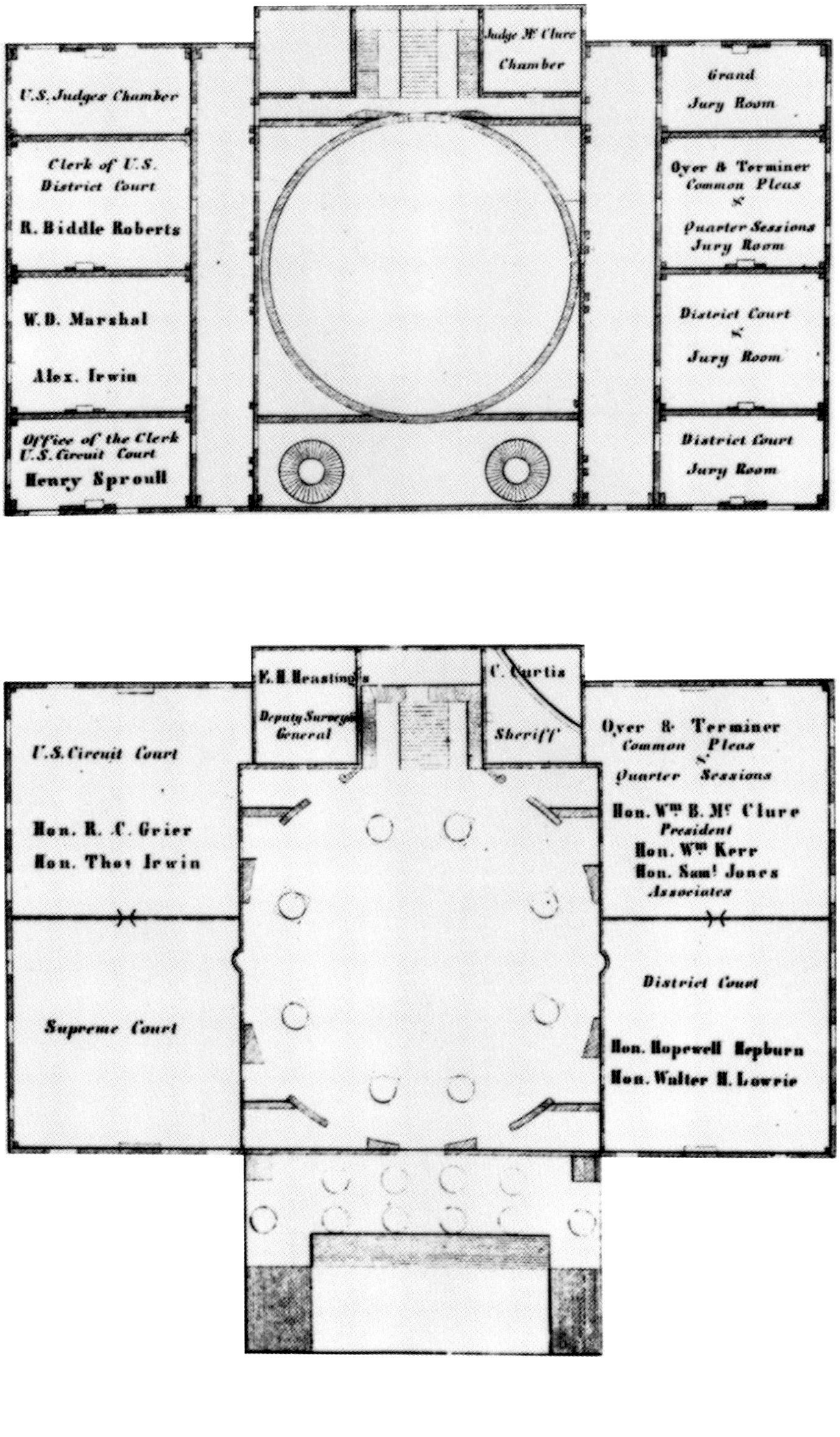

Plans of the second Court House, from Fahnestock's Pittsburgh Directory.

Pleas and Quarter Sessions), and the District Court. On either side of the main staircase at the back of the building were two offices, or perhaps jury rooms; they were smaller in dimension than the courtrooms, which were 45 feet square.

The third floor, according to Fahnestock, was dominated in the center by the upper part of the rotunda. Here a question arises as to the exact features of the Fahnestock plan. Was the great central ring the base of the dome, and where would this leave the Corinthian columns? Aside from this, however, the side of the structure toward Diamond Street was taken up by the various jury rooms of the courts below. On the Fifth Avenue side were the chambers of judges and offices of clerks. Both suites of rooms were reached by corridors on either side of the rotunda.

The Fahnestock plan for the basement shows the rotunda expressed by a ring of eight large square piers, presumably the podia for the Corinthian columns of the main floor. This great space, a circle within a square, is shown as open and accessible to the two corridors which gave access to the County offices housed on the Fifth Avenue and Diamond Street sides of the building. An account published in 1841 is probably the most accurate:

The basement contains eight rooms, four of which are thirty-two by twenty-five feet each. These are used for public offices; the prothonotary and recorder occupy the two in front, and the commissioners, clerk of sessions, etc., those in the rear. The whole of this story is made fireproof with groined arches and makes a safe depository for public records. These rooms are connected with each other by commodious passageways twelve feet in width.

Fahnestock shows no interior staircase on the basement plan; the space at the back of the rotunda on the first and second floors allocated to the accommodation of the main stairs is occupied below by two long narrow rooms labeled "water closets," (an indication that such facilities were part of the building in the 1840s). It is possible, however, that there may have been one or more small staircases connecting the basement with the floor above.

Coltart and Dilworth, the contractors for the second Court House, also built the new Jail. It was finished in 1837, and was briefly described in Harris' *Pittsburgh Business Directory for the Year 1837:*

The new Jail of Allegheny County is a large stone building on Grant's Hill on high ground commanding a good view of the city and suburbs. It is a strong secure edifice. In the front part facing the South there are two comfortable apartments for the families of the Sheriff and Jailer. There are six tiers of cells and ten cells to each tier, making in all sixty cells in the County prison.

There is little contemporary left in Pittsburgh now with which we can

Burke's Building (1836) by John Chislett. A city that 30 years before was still a borough with log houses was now building elegant stone-fronted business buildings such as this one, by a professional architect recently arrived from England.

compare the Doric austerities of the second Court House. Burke's Building on Fourth Avenue, with its central pavilion though minus a dome, is a miniature rendition of Chislett's Court House scheme. Here we have the same architectural elements: the heavy rusticated basement; the Doric porch (with only two columns in this case) with a pediment above; the severe, bland facade stretching upward and out. Even in looking at Burke's Building we can catch hints of the aging columns of the Court House, with their spalled and broken flutings, because the Fourth Avenue porch is in similar case. My office was once next door to Burke's Building, and often in the golden sunset of an autumn day or in the iron light of a grey winter morning I walked past the wonderful facade, faded and crumbling and robbed of its supporting buildings. At such times, almost nothing else being extant of the once-Greek city, I felt that it would be possible to reconstruct the Pittsburgh of the Revival from that one monument alone, such is its authority.

Curiously enough, the severe Doric mien long survived the Greek Revival in Pittsburgh, in some of the details of late nineteenth- and early twentieth-century Classical buildings. Of these, the most salient are the colossal screen of Doric columns on the main facade of the Frick Building (D. H. Burnham and Company, 1901-02), just across the street from the present Court House, and the engaged columns of the City-County

The second Court House around 1880, shortly before it burned. It now stood very high above Grant Street.

Building (Palmer, Hornbostel, and Jones, with Edward B. Lee, 1915-17). Sometimes it seems that the Doric column was the law-giver for much of Pittsburgh's architecture.

Like all large public buildings in America, the second Court House changed over the years. A building connecting the Jail and the Court House was constructed about 1861, and in a few decades the building itself had deteriorated. One history notes that

it was dark and dingy enough before its destruction by fire on 7 May 1882. The outer columns of soft sandstone had been broken at the edges of the flutings. . . and they presented a sorry appearance. The

> *lower floor of basement was damp and dingy and had a mouldy smell. Buildings of one story had been added on the Fifth Avenue side and also on the Diamond Street area until all the yard on that side had been occupied.*

Another source also describes the decayed condition of the second Court House:

> *Long before the Court House fire of 1882 the atmosphere had begun to wear away the stone perceptibly. So rapid was the corrosion in the air laden with coal smoke that the dressed surface of the front wall had dropped off, some of the cornices near the roof had begun to fall and the building had a general scaly look that would have rendered a new one necessary. All the building stone to be found in the Pittsburgh area has the same failing.*

Sic transit gloria mundi. Alas for Athens, Pittsburgh's Doric pride, and Solon's Dome. It had survived the Great Fire of April 1845 which had destroyed much of the city; but the constant sulphurous fumes of the local atmosphere ruined the Classic majesty of its face. As we see the Court House portrayed in 1874 in the romantic compendium *Picturesque America,* its domed presence is still impressive. The industrial fires of Pittsburgh had done their work, though. The life of the second Court House was limited.

Pittsburgh in 1874, seen from the north. The second Court House stands just to the right of center, with the towers of St. Paul's Cathedral close by. In the middle ground is the Allegheny River, with a suspension bridge of 1859 by John Augustus Roebling.

GRANT'S HILL, AND A FIRE

AN INTERLUDE

During the days of the second Court House, Grant's Hill kept changing. The steep slope of Grant's Hill came to be known as the "Hump," and the first cut made in 1836 resulted in a gradient of nine feet four inches to each hundred feet from Smithfield Street to Grant. The original gradient must have been extremely steep, considering that ten feet or more were removed and four feet filled in below. When the second large cut was made in 1847, the original plans called for a gradient of five feet four inches to each hundred feet. However the trustees of St. Paul's Church at Fifth and Grant objected: such a grading would ruin their building. The municipality adopted a compromise solution, making the gradient seven and forty-four hundredth's feet, which it remained until 1911.

About three years after the cut was made, the church caught fire on May 6, 1851 and was ruined. The chief reason for the destruction of the building was that the cuts in Grant's Hill had left the church on such a high embankment that firemen could not get water to the fire. When the new church was begun in the following year, the lot was dug away to the 1847 grade. A five-aisled Gothic structure was erected after the design of Thomas Walsh of New York, with Charles Bartberger of Pittsburgh as supervising architect. It was finished in 1855 and enlarged in 1870. This huge fantastic building, with its thin spiky towers and octagonal dome, was the near companion of the second and third Court Houses until it was demolished in 1904 to make way for the Union Arcade (now Two Mellon Bank Center).

St. Paul's Roman Catholic Cathedral, cater-cornered across Grant Street from the Court House, in a view of c. 1890.

Also in 1851-52, the Grant's Hill group of buildings was augmented at Grant and Diamond Streets, just across the street from the Court House. John Notman of Philadelphia designed the extremely handsome St. Peter's Episcopal Church, exemplifying the archaeological phase of the Gothic Revival. The simple stone broach spire of the "correctly designed" structure acted as a chaste footnote to the wild, dramatic turrets of St. Paul's Cathedral and the expansive dome of the Court House. Here also the Greek and Gothic aspects of revivaldom existed happily together until the ominous advent of the Frick Building at the beginning of the new century. Then St. Peter's was moved, stone by stone, to a new site in the Oakland district of Pittsburgh at Forbes and Craft Avenues, where it remains today.

In the mid-nineteenth century a tavern called the Oregon House stood on Grant Street where the City-County Building stands today. An old Pittsburgher once wrote:

> *The old Oregon House is associated in my mind with the general ''training days'' of old times. This sounds absurd: ''general training days'' in Pittsburgh in the '40s? . . . The town was then subjected to the customs made for the convenience and accommodation of the farmers.*
>
> *It was the custom for farmers to surrender a day to the state in lieu of a tax, and the citizens of the towns did likewise for many years after military service (in the militia) and regulations for maintaining the roads were modified or wholly changed.*
>
> *I have seen thousands of citizens, among them men of nearly every calling and profession except the clergy, assemble on the hill overlooking the Pennsylvania Railroad yards, elect a commander with due solemnity and after marching through the streets, reduce the commander to the ranks, or run him out of town.*
>
> *They were supplied with wooden swords and wooden guns. Such as preferred them carried broomsticks. As good-humored, jovial, motley a crowd as was ever seen, it was laughed at by the merchants as the procession passed along. Wooden cannons were preferred. Some preferred black faces, bonnets, and skirts. It was always a loud and boisterous mob. They were difficult to satisfy in the matter of music. The music was always paid in advance, but frequently the musicians discovered that their services could be dispensed with early in the day.*
>
> *When the ''general muster'' was held on the hill overlooking 15th and 16th Streets, the chief disturbers of the peace invariably halted at the Old Oregon House. Lying on the sward there or lolling on benches or chairs, crowding in the bar-room and pitching quoits in the rear of the house, hundreds contrived to pass the remainder of a jolly day. As the march was always up Fourth Street, the bar caught some customers on the upward movement, but it was the closing action that told heavily.*

Certainly, all these numerous secular activities were presided over by Solon's dome. After the middle of the century, the area became built up solidly. In 1854, the Western University of Pennsylvania bought a lot at the corner of Diamond and Ross Streets where it erected a building in 1856. This rather dull three-storied structure in the Italianate style served its purpose well enough, until it was bought in 1882 to serve as a temporary meeting place for the courts after the burning of the Court House.

At Fourth and Ross, the First Baptist Church was erected in 1867-76 after the design of David Gendell, a Philadelphia architect. Built in the manner of the mid-century Romanesque Revival, or Rundbogenstil, it had a large wheel window on its main facade flanked by two squat towers. It was demolished in 1909 to make way for the City-County Building.

An engraving of a sketch made from the top of the City Hall tower at Smithfield Street shows a very late view of the second Court House surrounded by the churchly towers. The dome and spires have a romantic mysterious air, more like those of a city seen in dreams. Perhaps it was a portent, for the Court House was soon to dissolve in fire and vanish forever.

All the Pittsburgh newspapers carried accounts of the fire of May 7, 1882. In the words of the *Commercial Gazette:*

At twenty minutes past twelve o'clock, when the streets were thronged by persons returning from the morning services of the several churches, smoke was noticed issuing from the dome of the immense pile which for so many years has stood on Grant's Hill. At first the sight, although unusual on any day and especially unusual on Sunday, did not attract much attention. But it continued to pour out in such a steady stream and with an increasing volume, so that in a few minutes it became evident that something was burning inside that demanded immediate attention. . . .

The engines of the district and Chief Evans responded instantly. When they arrived, no flames were visible, but smoke was pouring from every crevice of the roof and dome, and it needed but a moment for the Chief to comprehend that the services of the entire department would be required. A second, third, fourth, and fifth alarm were sent in from the same box the last being recorded at exactly half-past twelve o'clock, four minutes after the first alarm and then the firemen prepared to go to work, not knowing what was before them, but feeling instinctively that it would be a Herculean task. . . .

The fire fiend was [soon] *master of the situation. Nearly all of the engines in the city were on the ground, and assistance was coming from Allegheny, but it was evident that the fire was not to be restrained until it had spent its fury or progressed far enough to be fought with advantage. . . .*

By ten minutes past two the dome was swaying so violently that it was evident that its collapse could not long be delayed and a silence that was almost breathless fell upon the crowd. Every person got as far away as possible. . . . Finally the dome came down with a tremendous crash, the heavy weight at the base causing the greater

> *portion of the blazing mass to fall to the floor of the rotunda. With the dome's fall, the building assumed the appearance of a volcano, from the center of which sprang a solid mass of smoke, flame, and ashes at least fifty feet in diameter. . . .*
>
> *All that remained of the dome that a few hours before was visible from almost every quarter of the city was a large pile of charred timbers on the second floor of the rotunda. . . . The roof and third floor were completely destroyed, whilst the torrents of water thrown into the building from every direction poured into the court rooms and offices below, flooding them completely.*

So passed Solon's dome.

The fire marshal found no cause for the conflagration, but one witness said that a possible source might be a gas jet in a closet near the coffee stand. It is curious also that no day watchman was employed in the building on Sunday.

On the same date, the newspaper editorial stated:

> *The destruction of fire may indeed be, as some have suggested, a blessing in disguise as there is no telling how long it might otherwise have been suffered to remain. It might have fallen when crowded with people. . . . Every consideration of safety and economy points to the erection of a new Court House which will involve the expenditure of a million dollars more or less.*

First the green paradise, then Solon's dome and the Doric law-givers: now both were history! Something grander was to come, something that still remains with us to praise. And yet, as we look at the superb granite walls of the present Court House, we seem to see the shimmer of green leaves and the gleam of golden sandstone columns; perhaps we wish that we could have them still.

Ruins of the second Court House in the early 1880s.

THE PHOENIX TOWER

THE STORY OF ITS BUILDING, 1882-83

Six years after the destruction of the second Court House, a new, more solid, and grander one had risen from the ashes of the old. The splendid shaft of its tower soared upward, rising superior to the erstwhile dome. Although the authority of the dome as a governmental symbol was undiminished, henceforth the phoenix tower was to be the standard of Pittsburgh's municipal pride as well as the symbol of the law's majesty.

The County Commissioners, relates one account,

at once proceeded to rehabilitate the courts of law. . . . [The County authorities deserve more than a passing record.] *For while the new edifice will long remain a monument to the genius of the architect, the facts of its construction should, in this age of so much bargain and sale and official corruption true or charged, be a monument to the Commissioners under whom it was planned and built without the taxpayers having been burdened with a heavy debt or a whisper of corruption in its contracts, although the sum expended has been so great and the opportunities for what, in the political slang of the day, is called jobs, many.*

The Commissioners' first concern was to provide temporary quarters for the courts and County offices. This they did in two months' time by purchasing the Western University building for $80,000 and erecting another structure at a cost of $43,000. Meanwhile, they had not been idle in clearing away the ruins:

The Ross Street home of the Western University of Pennsylvania. Built in 1854-55, it was purchased in 1882 by the County as its emergency quarters.

[T]*he Commissioners. . . passed a resolution instructing the County Engineer to prepare plans for the separation and removal of the damaged part of the Court House building and for the grading of the portion of the lot on which it stood down to the level of Grant and Diamond Streets.*

Their *Minutes* also say:

The City of Pittsburgh was heavily burdened with the indebtedness as were other sections of the County and it was desirable that an increase of taxation should be avoided.

But the duty of providing suitable accommodations for the courts and county officers was imperative and required prompt action. As was to be expected under the circumstances, much honest difference of opinion existed among the citizens and taxpayers as to what was best to be done. . . . Many thought that in view of the heavy public burdens it would be better to let the Jail and the undamaged portion of the Court House building stand and to build an addition to it.

Others contended that the Jail was badly located and in many respects inadequate to the public wants, and that in order to make provision for the present and prospective wants of the County, all the old buildings should be removed and a new Court House erected in size covering the entire lot.

In the latter opinion the Commissioners concurred.

On June 4th, 1882 they presented their petition to the Grand Jury, sitting at the June Sessions, that they contemplated "the erection of such buildings as might be necessary for the accommodations of the courts and the several officers of the County and for the reception and safe keeping of the records and papers in charge of such officers; and also such building as might be necessary and proper for the purposes of a County Jail to be erected on ground to be purchased for that purpose; the said contemplated improvements having been rendered essential and necessary by reason of the destruction of the Court House by the recent fire and the prospective increase of the population and business of the County. . . .

"We are deeply impressed with the necessity of the exercise of such rigid economy in the re-erection of the public buildings as is consistent with durability and convenience and with the safety of the public records. We have examined carefully and are of the opinion that much of the material in and about the Court House which was burned particularly the stones in the wall and in the wall around the yard and perhaps other material can be used to good advantage in rebuilding. . . . And in case it shall be decided to rebuild with stone, no new stone will be required except such as may be needed for the outside course of the outer walls. We therefore think it injudicious to sell the material in the Court House and buy new material for the walls, flagging, etc. . . .

"With the foregoing expression of our views, we approve of the contemplated re-erection of the Court House and offices, and recommend that work be commenced and prosecuted as speedily as may be consistent with its being well and economically done. . . ."

During [the latter part of 1882 and early 1883] *many taxpayers grew impatient. Daily the question was asked. "What is being done toward building a Court House?" . . . The Commissioners anticipat-*

ing the approval of the Court. . . set about to procure information relative to the erection of buildings of the size and character required. With this purpose they visited many Court Houses and other public buildings which had been recently erected.

Upon this trip Mr. Charles Davis, the County Engineer, accompanied them, made notes of their observations and with his assistance they gleaned much information in relation to material, plan of construction, mode of heating and ventilating as well as the defects and mistakes of others.

The *Minutes* state that this trip took place in December 1882, but this must be in error because the *Commercial Gazette* reported the results of the journey, beginning with their issue of August 28:

The County Commissioners and County Engineer Davis have at length found a model for the proposed new Court House. They returned on Saturday after an extended trip of ten days devoted to the inspection of public buildings at Indianapolis, Chicago, Detroit, Buffalo, Albany, Philadelphia, Washington, and other cities. The model of a building that most suited their fancy was the Court House at Buffalo, New York. . . . At Washington, D.C. the County Engineer received some valuable information as to heating and ventilation, a report of which will be submitted to the County Prison Board. U.S.

City and County Hall, Buffalo, 1871-76, by Andrew Jackson Warner. The County Commissioners apparently liked this building best of the many they saw. The corner pavilions and central tower follow a compositional formula, common at the time, that all the competitors for the Allegheny County Court House would use. The style, unusual in 1871, is Romanesque.

> *Government architect Walters also informed the engineer that the material best suited for building in the sulphuric atmosphere of Pittsburgh is a good quality granite and recommended Quincy granite of sombre shade.*

On August 29, 1882, the *Commercial Gazette* reported:

> *Mr. Davis said that the trip of the Commissioners was not ''intended as an exploration for a model building but rather to learn the advantages and disadvantages of other public building as regards hearing and ventilating, simplicity, and acoustic properties that only the best points could be used in the construction of the building for the transaction of the County's legal business. . . .*
>
> *''We inspected a number of buildings that embraced several essentials of a courthouse for this County, but found none that completely would serve as a model. . . . It has been so published, but I do not believe the Commissioners will recommend the* [Buffalo] *building as a model. . . .''*
>
> *When asked of what the new building would be constructed, Davis replied, ''Quincy granite has been recommended, but we would like to have an entirely fireproof building and one constructed of granite is not the best to withstand fire. Brick is the best material when the fire question is taken into consideration. A combination of the two, however, would be desirable.''*
>
> *''When will the Commissioners make a report and when will we hear of something being done toward the erection of the new courthouse?. . .''*
>
> *''The County Commissioners are not in a hurry and will make no report until they know whereof they speak. They will thoroughly examine every point before that time, and the public will know in good time.''*
>
> *With the concluding remark that a very good building could be constructed for a million dollars, Mr. Davis walked away.*

Finally the *Commercial Gazette* editorialized on August 30,

> *For the present, however, it is sufficiently clear that a million dollars carefully expended will furnish full and commodious offices for the County buildings and give us a building surpassing in architectural attraction anything that Pittsburgh has ever had. That being the case a million dollars is all that Allegheny County can afford to expend and the authorities in charge should see that the plans are kept within that amount.*

There is in all this something portentous: one begins to feel, as in the opening bars of a great symphony or in a high drama, the introductory parleyings among the servants, a sense of inevitability, in these deliberations, these searchings, this dedication. Gradually, the feeling mounts that some superb climax is coming, something extraordinary, magnificent beyond words, will result. The phoenix tower had its heralds and forerunners who announced its superior beauty, its municipal and its supernal function.

January 1883 opened with discussions concerning a new jail. On New Year's Day the *Commercial Gazette* wrote, "There has been considerable talk about shutting down the old jail building and erecting a new one to correspond with the new Court House. . . . All the County Commissioners and the judges are said to favor the erection of a new jail." According to the Pittsburgh *Weekly Chronicle* of January 20, 1883,

the County Prison Society held their annual meeting Wednesday evening. The report on the County prison was presented by Rev. E. R. Donohoo. Among other things the Committee report that "until a jail is erected with cells sufficient in number and so constructed as to secure perfect isolation for each prisoner held for trial, only the saddest results need be expected from such an uncivilized method of dealing with those who by misfortune, temptation, or depravity have been subjected to such unavoidable abuses as are now of necessity tolerated in the name of law and justice."

The official report declares,

On February 10, 1883, the board of Prison Inspectors of Allegheny County by resolution requested that the Commissioners submit to them a report in relation to the erection of the new buildings.

On February 12, 1883, the report was submitted and copies of it were at once printed and distributed among the citizens of the County.

The bulk of this pamphlet, which is introduced by the Commissioners' foreword, consists of a report by County Engineer Charles Davis. He listed the buildings visited by the Commissioners and gave a brief description of each of these structures. The concluding pages of the pamphlet are concerned with the recommendations of the Commissioners for the new County Buildings at Pittsburgh.

The report sets forth "that the public think that the erection of new buildings should be begun promptly. Believing that such is the public sentiment, and knowing that it will take much longer time to mature plans and designs than most persons suppose, and that the designs and plans must be completed and full in detail in order that an approximate estimate of cost can be procured before a move is made toward erection, we have thought it advisable to anticipate the approval of the Court."

The report closes with a request for any information, advice, or suggestions which may be helpful in aiding and guiding in the performance of the work.

Upon the filing of this report it was evident that the erection of new buildings involving a large expenditure was determined upon by the Commissioners and that they preferred granite for use in the outer walls.

Whilst the course contemplated was endorsed by some, more earnestness and feeling were displayed opposing it. Each class of material, iron, sandstone, limestone, and brick had its advocates who opposed the use of granite, whilst others opposed any plan which would have necessitated a large outlay of money. The public press discussed and voiced the different opinions which were set forth.

Before the Commissioners approached any architects for plans and proposals, they consulted with all the County officials "as to what each would need or desire as to room or wall space in their respective offices." Among the Commissioners' recommendations were the following:

> *The building in its general appearance should suggest the purpose for which it is intended. It should be characterized by solidity and dignity of design and simplicity of decoration. Elaborate or intricately carved work for the exterior would soon be obscured or defaced by soot accumulations and the action of the weather. The floor should be of iron beams and brick or tile arches and the beams should be covered with fireproof material where exposed. Iron windows and door jambs should be used, and for the most part of the interior finish should be marble, iron or other indestructible material. . . . The roof should be iron covered with slate and tile.*

The Commissioners' *Minutes* state:

> *At a special meeting of the County Commissioners held this April 16, 1883 the board passed the following—*
>
> *Resolved. That the Clerk is hereby authorized to have one hundred copies of the following letter of enquiry printed in script for the purpose of being addressed to such architects as may in the judgement of the County Commissioners be deemed advisable.*
>
> *Respected Sir:*
>
> *The destruction of our County Building by fire in May, last, makes it necessary for us to take steps looking to the erection of a new one at any early date. Under these circumstances we address you and a number of other Architects the following interrogations:*
>
> *Will you be willing to make a study of this proposed building and furnish us with the following preliminary drawings:*
>
> *(1) A plan of each of the several stories*
>
> *(2) Front and side elevations*

(3) Longitudinal and Transverse sections, including other necessary details

(4) Perspective view of the exterior.

The said plans and drawings to be accompanied with a full description of the same, (including the method you propose for making the building fireproof, and an explanation of any special features you may introduce) with skeleton specifications and an estimate of cost of such building completed, in accordance with your design.

All drawings to be on a scale of one-eighth (1/8) of inch to one foot and finished in ink except the perspective which shall be finished in sepia tints. . . .

How soon can you complete and deliver the aforesaid work and what compensation will you require for the same?

Our views as to the character and dimensions of the proposed structure and the accommodation required are fully set forth in a pamphlet, a copy of which has already been sent to you by mail.

We shall be pleased if you favor us with an early reply.

R. E. Mercer
Daniel McWilliams
George Y. McKee, County Commissioners

The *Commercial Gazette* on April 28, 1883 reported that "since the County Commissioners sent out their circular letter to architects. . . a large number of replies have been received from architects of various cities. Some of those addressed have paid a personal visit to the Commissioners to consult about the matter, and today they will see one of the most prominent architects in the country."

The Commissioners' *Minutes* continue:

Many of the answers were evasive and unsatisfactory. The architects who answered differed in time required for making preliminary studies from one month to twelve and in their charges for studies from three hundred dollars to thirty thousand dollars.

On September 8, 1883 the Commissioners resolved that the sum of twenty-five hundred dollars be offered to each of five architects, to prepare studies of the proposed new buildings in accordance with the requirements contained in the circular letter sent out in April, 1883, the studies to be submitted to the Board on January 1st, 1884, and to become the property of the County.

George Henry Thurston writes that "one of these architects was to be a resident of Allegheny County, two residents in the Eastern States and two in the Western." The architects chosen were Andrew Peebles of Pittsburgh, John Ord of Philadelphia, George B. Post of New York,

William W. Boyington of Chicago, and Elijah E. Myers of Detroit. All agreed to compete except Post.

Andrew Peebles was the only Pittsburgher, a Scot who had come to the city by way of Canada. We do not know his birth and death dates, but he was active in Pittsburgh between 1871 and 1896. By 1880 he had a busy local practice, and by the end of his career he had designed a number of important commercial buildings and churches. St. Peter's R.C. Church (1874) on the North Side and the First Lutheran Church (1886-88) on Grant Street are two surviving works. As a local man, he may have used some influence to be admitted to the competition. We do not know what his ideas were for the Court House, and indeed it is not literally true that he competed; he was eventually excluded for being behind with his plans.

John Ord (fl. 1880) was another Scot, who was practising in Philadelphia where he had earned quite a reputation. He seems to have been active at least into the 1890s.

William W. Boyington (1818-98) was a Chicago architect, well known nationally. Self-educated, he was intensely busy in the decades before and after the Chicago Fire of 1871. The famous Water Tower (1869) that still survives is a Boyington design; so were the third Board of Trade Building (1882) and the Grand Pacific Hotel (burned 1871 on completion, rebuilt 1873).

Elijah E. Myers (1832-1909) was a Detroit practitioner of national fame. A specialist in state capitols, court houses, and other official buildings,

Below: St. Peter's (R.C.) Church, Allegheny, 1872-74, by Andrew Peebles. The tower originally carried a tall spire.

Below right: The Triangle Building, Pittsburgh, 1884, by Andrew Peebles. The two upper floors, much plainer than the Victorian Gothic below, are an addition of the 1890s.

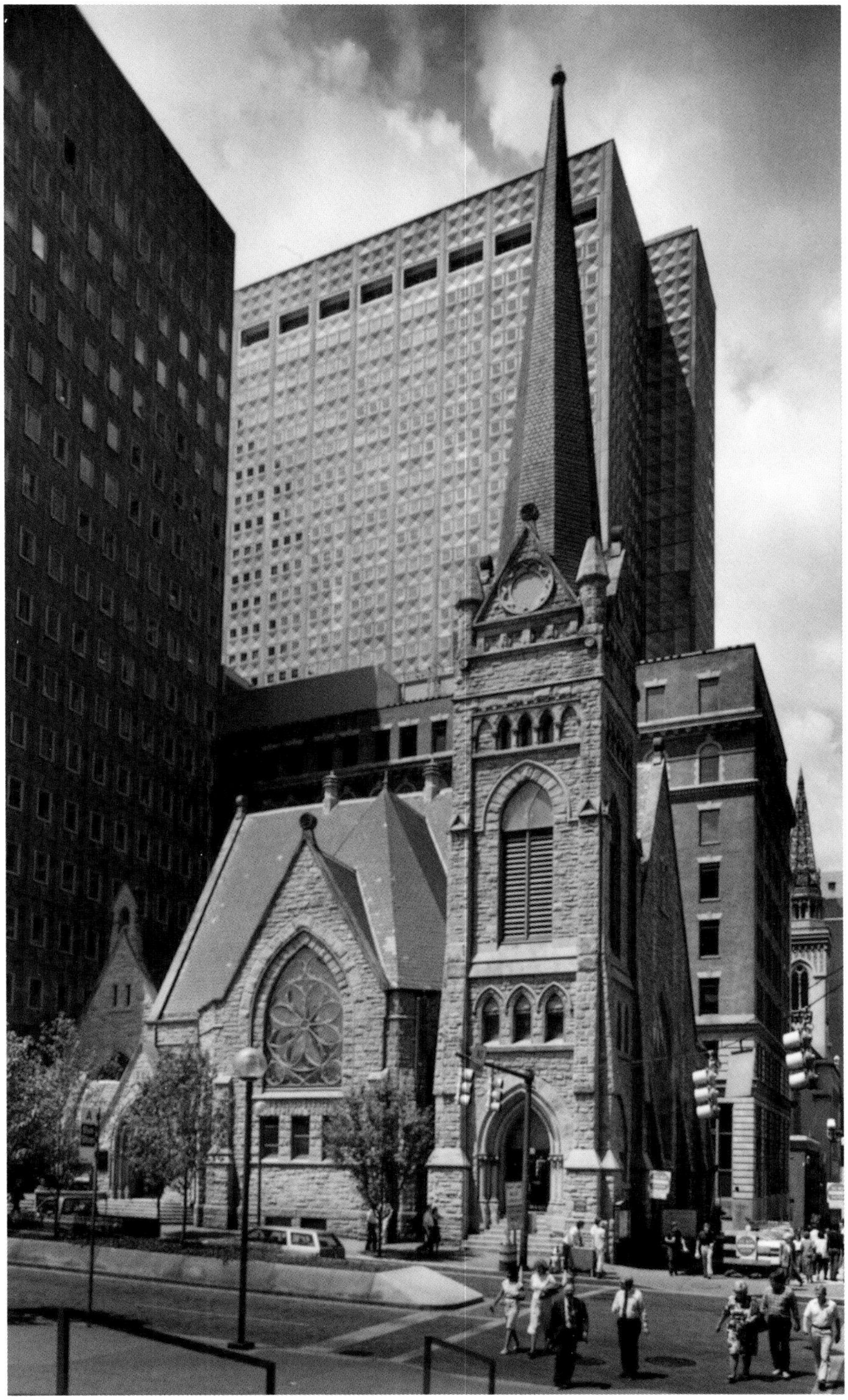

First Lutheran Church, Pittsburgh, 1887-88, by Andrew Peebles.

he had job-getting and job-doing down to a near-science. The Michigan, Texas, and Colorado capitols are his.

And finally is the architect who originally had no intention of competing. . . but who won: Henry Hobson Richardson (1838-86).

Edwin Hetherington continues the story:

> *Henry Hobson Richardson was not among these five because no reply to the April letter had been received. Perhaps his office was too busy in the spring and summer of 1883 to consider seriously a large project like the Court House and Jail. In late March he was finishing his elaborate studies for All Saints' Cathedral in Albany, a competition he dearly hoped to win. When his plans were rejected in early May, he probably turned with renewed vigor to the completion of drawings for the west facade of Trinity Church in Boston. At this time Richardson was still working on the New York State Capitol in Albany, Austin Hall at Cambridge, as well as some houses. More recent works included the Billings Library in Burlington, Vermont (April, 1883), the Converse Library in Malden, Massachusetts (August, 1883) and the Emmanuel Episcopal Church in Allegheny City, Pennsylvania (August, 1883).*
>
> *It is very likely because of this last commission that Richardson was invited to participate in the Court House and Jail competition. After the original five were chosen in early September a group of prominent citizens expressed their interest in the Boston architect. Probably this group was composed of parishioners or vestrymen from Emmanuel Church who had just a few weeks earlier asked Richardson to design a new building. The Emmanuel parish in Allegheny City (now part of Pittsburgh's North Side) included one of the County's most exclusive residential areas, and thus it seems plausible that the Commissioners would have appreciated the favorable opinion of this particular group. After George B. Post* [a well-known New York architect with a large commercial practice] *refused the County's offer, Richardson became the fifth architect on 28 September, 1883.*
>
> *It is interesting to note that Richardson replaced Post in the competition, much as he had taken the latter's position in the New York architectural partnership of Gambrill and Post in October, 1867. Similarly, just as the Church of Unity in Springfield, Massachusetts gave Richardson the chance to begin his career, so also did Emmanuel Church give him the opportunity to build* [in Pittsburgh] *one of his best works.*

Although there is still no positive proof that the members of Emmanuel Episcopal Church helped ensure Richardson that chance to compete for the County Buildings, there is a strong probability of some connection, since the case for Emmanuel has been so persuasively asserted

Above: Henry Hobson Richardson's unexecuted design of 1882-83 for All Saints Episcopal Cathedral, Albany.

Left: Henry Hobson Richardson's Emmanuel Episcopal Church, Allegheny, 1886. This replaced his earlier and more elaborate design, rejected on account of cost, and relied principally on massing and decorative brick bonding for its effect.

by Mr. Hetherington. Mrs. Van Rensselaer, author of *Henry Hobson Richardson and His Works* (1888), writes that Richardson, "was especially proud of the chance to build [the County Buildings] as the invitation had come from so distant a spot and had been prompted by the sight of his works alone and not by a personal acquaintance of any member of the committee with himself." Possibly the Commissioners did know Richardson only by reputation; through their journeyings; they had seen his Capitol and City Hall at Albany. Nevertheless, a chance piece of information I received tends to confirm Hetherington's surmise. Young New Englanders in the nineteenth century often went "west" to improve their prospects. Such a young man was John Howland Ricketson, who had been in Richardson's graduating class at Harvard. According to John Howland Ricketson III, his great-grandfather had come to Pittsburgh and married into the Garrison family, well known in local industry, and it was he who had suggested that Richardson be asked to join in the competition. Richardson was a man of great personal charm, and the friends of his youth at Harvard are known to have helped him. Despite a lack of documentary evidence, this seems the most probable reason for his inclusion. It is interesting that Emmanuel Church was at no great distance from Ricketson's house, though Ricketson attended St. Andrew's Church, on Ninth Street in Pittsburgh. (With all his charm, Richardson annoyed Mrs. Ricketson; he often stayed at the Ricketson house on his Pittsburgh visits and would commandeer the family brougham without asking permission.) Another account records that:

> *the moment the opportunity to build the Pittsburgh Court House was offered to* [Richardson] *he grasped it with delight, as the great opportunity of his life. But he did not seize it as a chance to show his art in ornamental work, or in erecting a large Court House wholly of his own design. No man ever evinced a greater aversion to being hampered or cramped in his conceptions than did Mr. Richardson, but he did not regard these directions* [the Commissioners' recommendations issued with the first circular letter to the architects] *as restrictions. He quickly perceived that the requirements given should be appropriate for its intended use. . . .*
>
> *When Mr. Richardson reached Pittsburgh, his first act was to call upon the Commissioners. He entered their office with a copy of the instructions sent out by them in his hand, elegantly rebound. It was their first meeting. After introductions had passed, Mr. Richardson expressed his high appreciation of the instructions given to the architects. He said he regarded them as a model of their kind; that he had never seen either in this country or in Europe, instructions presented by any building committee which set forth so fully and explicitly the requirements for the intended work, and while his attention had been called to this work, he had not thought of giving*

Rear of the Albany City Hall, as built. The rendering on the next page shows the stone footbridge originally planned.

City Hall, Albany, 1880-82, by Henry Hobson Richardson. The massing is less formal than it was to be at Pittsburgh, but the walls have an open character that was to be repeated in the Court House competition design. Beside the Pittsburgh tower, that at Albany has a delicate character.

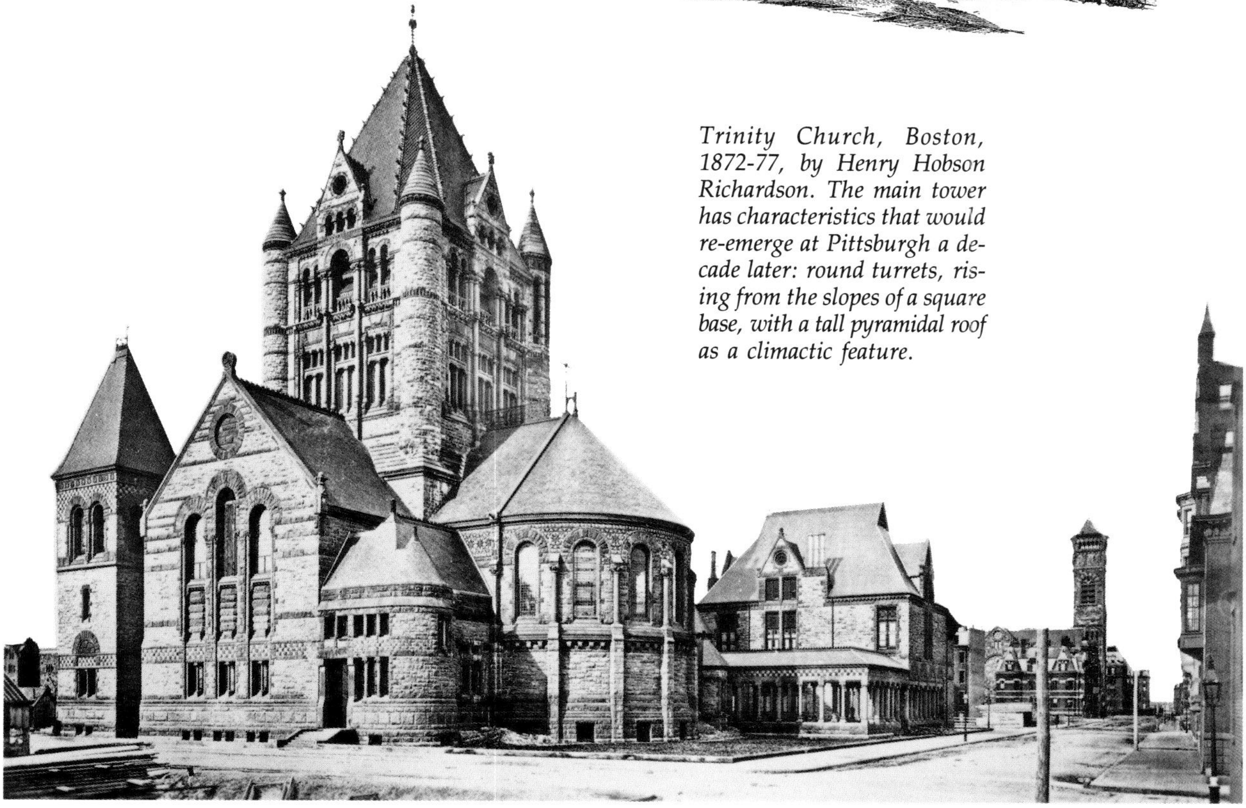

Trinity Church, Boston, 1872-77, by Henry Hobson Richardson. The main tower has characteristics that would re-emerge at Pittsburgh a decade later: round turrets, rising from the slopes of a square base, with a tall pyramidal roof as a climactic feature.

it any consideration until he saw the instructions.

It is evident that the long and close association between the Commissioners and Richardson (which lasted until his death in 1886) was initiated at this interview.

Henry Hobson Richardson was born in Louisiana. During his youth he planned to attend West Point; however, he was rejected because of a slight stammer in his speech. Instead, Richardson enrolled at Harvard in the Class of 1859. There his original ambition was to be a civil engineer, but by the end of college he had decided to study architecture. His family sent him to the Ecole Nationale des Beaux-Arts in Paris, then regarded as having the world's best school of architecture. He began there as a well-to-do young American of great promise, but the outbreak of the Civil War put an end to both the stipends from home and his certainty about continuing his studies. Richardson returned to Boston in 1862, where he had friends (he made and kept friends wherever he went). However, he could find no work in Boston and he was not able to reach his hometown of New Orleans, so he returned to Paris. There Richardson lived in comparative poverty until the Civil War ended. He was then faced with a quandary; his family wanted him back in Louisiana, his Parisian friends wanted him to stay on and become a French subject; he, on the other hand, wanted to go back to America but to a city with more promise for his career than one in the exhausted South. The result was that Richardson settled in New York, and later in the Boston area.

Very truly Yours
H. H. Richardson

His first real chance to prove his architectural talent was in designing, in 1866, a Unitarian church at Springfield, Massachusetts. His Brattle Square Church (1870) in the smart new Back Bay section of Boston gave him his first real fame and was the first indication of his mature powers. In 1872 Richardson was invited to compete for Trinity Church, a few blocks away. He and his draftsman Stanford White (soon to be famous himself) created a church that not only broke neatly with the rather arid manner of Mid-Victorian architecture but attempted, as seldom before in America, to combine painting and sculpture with architecture into an integrated work of art; this integration would soon be all but mandatory in monumental construction. After Trinity, one work rapidly followed another: stores, houses, libraries, railroad stations, an occasional church. By the mid-1880s his Romanesque style was fashionable; Chicago, St. Paul, Boston, and eventually Pittsburgh could testify to his acclaim. In addition, Richardson was an able, straightforward designer in the Shingle Style, using the old native siding along with native stone to create big, sheltering country houses.

Opposite: Henry Hobson Richardson around 1883, dressed as a monk for this photograph by George Collins Cox.

Taxed by a vigorous working schedule, Richardson was obliged to travel in 1882 to restore his health. Since he chose to vacation in southern Europe, the home ground of the Romanesque style he favored, the trip was often far from leisurely. Richardson returned revived (if not improved

in health) with memories that inspired him for four more years.

Richardson had Bright's disease, and changed from the rather gaunt person he had been at Harvard to a rotund, majestic figure of some 300 pounds (One Victorian dared to say that Richardson looked like his buildings.) Photos taken in 1883, perhaps as a stunt, show Richardson in a monk's gown, thoughtful over his work. His grand appearance in fact resulted from abnormal retention of water. Richardson died from his disease in 1886. The successor firm of Shepley, Rutan and Coolidge completed the work then on the drawing boards (our new Court House and Jail included) and continued to accept new commissions, which they fulfilled with polish.

Richardson was an ambiguous figure in the history of American architecture. On the one hand, he has been taken as a proto-Modernist and one of a type dear to the American temperament. He created bold arches, used natural materials in their rough form, and attacked commercial and industrial problems—though the latter quite peripherally—with style and grace. But doctrinaire Modernists cannot quite forgive the presence of ornament in his work, and are rather inclined to slight his more elaborate works in favor of the consciously simple Allegheny County Jail and Marshall Field Building (Chicago, 1885; now gone).

Richardson was a leader in a time that worried about the historic truth of the architecture it was producing, that wanted something identifiable of its place and time, but that was not committed to total originality and that was attempting rather to revive old standards. The integration of genuinely good painting, sculpture, mosaic, and stained glass with architecture, the revival of then decadent crafts, and the improvement of professional standards were major concerns of Richardson and his colleagues. Richardson collected an architectural library that served as cribs for the more passive intellects of his draftsmen. His guiding technique was to create the general design concept; then his draftsmen would leaf through his books, work under his supervision, and refine the design. This gave Richardson the time he needed for travel, conferences, and rest. He was available often enough to guide the work, at least until toward the end of his life. His draftsmen were not mere employees, but were treated as gentlemen who had come to him to learn. He ran a loyal and happy studio from his (non-Richardson) house in Brookline, near Boston. Here he lived a cheerful, hospitable, hedonistic existence as time and health permitted. His friends were the American aristocracy of wealth and/or pedigree.

Richardson was not a radical, but rather a man who was attempting to revive values the Mid-Victorian age had allowed to lapse, and to integrate those values gracefully with the complex demands of a capitalist industrial civilization.

Once Richardson died, it was possible for the sensitive architectural observer to miss him acutely. For Romanesque stayed in fashion, and

Above: the Marshall Field Wholesale Store, Chicago, 1885-87, by Henry Hobson Richardson. The walls are solid masonry, with large window areas to admit maximum air and light. Its much simpler plan and humbler uses did not require the monumental treatment and strong articulation of the contemporary Court House, but architectural historians give it equal respect.

Left: Henry Hobson Richardson's study and library at Brookline, Massachusetts, c. 1886, with the cultured clutter enjoyed by the late Victorian aesthete. On the desk is Richardson's portrait in monk's costume.

while some designers worked quite respectably, and now and then powerfully, in his style, most did not. In a poor attempt to imitate Richardson, every builder around 1890 toned up his work with a four-inch veneer of rugged masonry. By 1895 the popularity of Richardson Romanesque had faded, and by 1905 only very backward architects used the style.

The work on the competition drawings went on at a rapid pace during the remaining months of 1883. On December 22, 1883, the *Commercial Gazette* reported:

> *By January all the plans for the new Court House that are now being prepared. . . will be in the hands of the County Commissioners who are preparing to publicly exhibit them. . . . The plans will be complete and models of workmanship. Each architect, in accepting his election was told who the five chosen architects were, and each is trying to excel the others. Mr. Richardson the architect from Boston told the County Commissioners a few days ago that his plans have already cost him $3,000. He has had 20 experienced draftsman at work for three months. The contract price of the plans was $2,500.*

The plans as finally submitted by Richardson ''cost him more than twice the sum offered to be paid by the County.''

In the new year, 1884, the first versions of the phoenix tower were to be placed on view.

By contrast, the drafting room had a plain and almost improvised look. To the left, in the rear, is a rendering of the Marshall Field Wholesale Store; in the center a draftsman is working on an elevation, probably for the Cincinnati Chamber of Commerce.

THE PHOENIX TOWER

THE STORY OF ITS BUILDING
JANUARY—JUNE 1884

As the year opened and the curtain rose once again on the Court House drama, there was considerable activity in anticipation of the exposition of the drawings of the competing architects.

The architects were arriving in Pittsburgh. The *Daily Post* for January 1, 1884 reported that "Colonel E. E. Meyers [sic] arrived in Pittsburgh with plans for the Court House and Jail." On January 3, the *Pittsburgh Times* stated that "Mr. Richardson spent the afternoon Saturday with the County Commissioners and County Engineer Davis explaining his designs to them, and had the opportunity to compare his work with that of Myers. Peebles of Pittsburgh did not have his plans ready at the specified time so he was disqualified."

Although we have no way of knowing, Andrew Peebles may not have been displeased with his disqualification. He had plenty of "small" work in Pittsburgh, and it must have been evident that he was not used to competing with nationally-famous architects. He probably entered the competition as a concession to local pride. To speak truth, there was almost certainly no office in Pittsburgh in 1884 that could have physically encompassed a commission of this magnitude. This was to change, with the Richardson-trained men who invaded the city in the wake of the great architect. The competition for the Carnegie Institute commission of 1891 was to be quite another story. Longfellow, Alden and Harlow won where Peebles failed honorably; but they won because of Richardson.

Surely the County Commissioners bowed respectfully—if ever so slightly—in the direction of Pittsburgh and Peebles, and then turned their attention to the other competitors.

The exhibition hall for the competition drawings was selected and made ready. According to the *Commercial Gazette* of January 4, 1884:

Workmen were busy yesterday arranging the Old Welsh Church for the exhibition of the plans of the new Court House submitted to the Commissioners by the architects employed. . . . The Commissioners

> *were under no obligation to employ as supervising architect the man whose plan should be adopted; . . . they had simply contracted with the architects to furnish plans, but. . . they were free to reject any or all plans, or* [to] *select some other architect to supervise the erection of the building.*

We have descriptions of the plans of Richardson's competitors:

> *The Meyers* [sic] *plan is one which visualizes the Court House in the Corinthian style. It will have three stories and a basement. To be built of smooth cut granite, the interior is somewhat similar to Richardson's plan. Meyers' dimensions are 208 x 300 feet with a height of 122 feet. The tower would be 290 feet high. The estimated cost of this structure is $1,813,636.35. The jail done in a massive style of architecture will have a tower on Ross Street, 318 cells, and will be connected to the Court House by a tunnel under Ross Street.*

On January 5, the newspaper continued, "The plans for the new Court House prepared by architect Boyington of Chicago were opened yesterday. His plan shows a handsome building covering the entire square, of the Renaissance style of architecture, to be built of granite. It is four stories high." And on January 10:

> *The plans submitted by Mr. Ord show a handsome building in the "free classic" style of architecture. It is four stories high and is surmounted by a clock tower. The dimensions of the building are 303 feet in length and 209 feet in width, with an interior court 126 feet by 90 feet. The principal entrance is on Grant Street and the upper floors are reached by four broad stairways at the angles, and four elevators.*

When the exhibition of drawings was thrown open to the public, it was thronged by all classes of Pittsburgh citizens and, as a contemporary said,

> *many. . . after several examinations of the drawings visited the Commissioners and spoke in favor of the plans they preferred. The best civil and mechanical engineers and most prominent manufacturers criticized the plans and gave their opinion as to the strength of the walls and other matters pertaining to the solidity, durability, architectural beauty, and adaptability of the edifice for the purpose for which it was intended.*

The drawings by Myers, Boyington, and Ord have survived and have been exhibited. Printed explanations of both Ord's and Myers' projects can be found in the Carnegie Library of Pittsburgh. A complete set of Richardson's designs, photographically reproduced, exists in the Bureau of Records of the County Works Department in Pittsburgh. These,

Elijah E. Myers' submission. The Court House is in a rather plain Second Empire style, while the Jail combines Gothic romance in rusticated stone with industrial utilitarianism in brick.

William W. Boyington's Court House, in a sort of Classicized Romanesque.

John Ord's facade, with its corner turrets and curved gables, uses Renaissance chateau motifs introduced to American architecture only a few years before.

together with Richardson's final working drawings (also in Pittsburgh) and the numerous sketches and studies at the Houghton Library in Harvard, give us a fairly complete overview of the design phase of the County Buildings. Also to be found at the Houghton Library is the only known copy of Richardson's printed explanation of his drawings.

Richardson begins his description by formally addressing the three Allegheny County Commissioners:

> *I have the honor to submit for your consideration the accompanying series of drawings, presenting plans, sections, elevations, and perspective views of your proposed Court House. The following pages are designed to aid in making their intention clear to you by a verbal description:*
>
> ***First****, of the arrangements purely of convenience with regard to the business of the courts;*
>
> ***Second****, of the arrangements for securing an abundant and pure supply of air, for regulating the temperature, and for admitting light;*
>
> ***Third****, of the design with regard to suitability of architectural effect. . . .*
>
> ***THE PLAN*** *of the building is strictly utilitarian, the aim being to obtain the greatest practicable advantages for its distinctive purposes that can be had within reasonable limits of outlay. In considering what is reasonable in this respect the structure has been regarded as one of permanent character, and the probabilities of an enlarged population and an advancing standard of civilized requirement have not been overlooked.*
>
> ***AS TO LIGHT****, the object has been to overcome local disadvantages by making as large window spaces as shall be consistent with due strength of walls, and by restoring to special expedients of which the result will be that the court rooms and all the principal offices receive floods of light from* two sides, *while not a single room in the building lacks direct light through the outer walls in excess of ordinary rules.*
>
> ***WITH REGARD TO AIR****, an abundant supply is to be drawn from an elevation at which it will be free from the heavier gases, and this supply is to be screened and purified before it is thrown into the working departments.*
>
> ***AS TO ARCHITECTURAL EFFECT****, with the atmospheric difficulties of the locality in view, the design has been to provide a building the character of which should depend on its outlines, on the massing and accentuation of the main features representing its leading purposes, and on the relation of the openings to the solid parts. Although, under your requirements, a great preponderance of openings is necessary, the intention has been to produce that sense of solidity requisite in dignified, monumental work, by a careful study*

of the piers and by a quiet and massive treatment of the wall surfaces. In accordance with this policy, projecting string-courses and cornices, and elaborate capitals and carvings, are as much as possible avoided, and no dependence for architectural effect is placed upon features liable to be distorted by soot.

[The plan, as originally laid out, is given in minute detail.]

THE CONSTRUCTION [the description then continues] *is fireproof throughout. The outer walls on the street are of granite backed with brick; those facing the court yard are of brick with granite trimmings* [in execution, a complete granite facing was laid.] *The main division walls are of brick, the other party walls of fireproof material; all brick walls are covered with a coat of tar to prevent sweat-*

Henry Hobson Richardson's competition design for the Court House differed notably from the executed work in the more open character of the walls and the placing of the tower away from the Grant Street front. Other details differ as well to give this version a lighter, less reposeful character.

The grand stair of the Court House in the 1884 design.

ing, and are then lined with a furring of fireproof material, commonly known as breeze, *on which plaster is laid. The ceilings of the main entrance hall and the grand staircase hall in the second story are vaulted.* [In execution, the vaulting of the stair hall was of brick between iron beams—standard heavy construction of the period—while the entrance hall had stone groin vaulting.] *The floors otherwise are of fireproof arch-blocks supported on iron beams. All the floors are leveled with concrete; above the concrete is a layer of asphalt, which makes the floors water-proof as well as fireproof. The roofs of the towers are of stone; the other roofs are of iron covered with black slate.* [In execution, red shingle tile was used.] *The window casings and frames are of iron. Iron cases of waterproof construction for records are provided in all of the offices of record. In the construction of the walls of both the sub-basement and the basement, the greatest care has been taken to provide against the spread of dampness in either a horizontal or a vertical direction. . . .*

[The great tower was not only a symbol but also a place for archival storage; and his description of the heating and ventilation shows that it was intended as the intake for a kind of air-conditioning system made desirable, like the granite facing, by the Pittsburgh atmosphere.]

The supply of air is drawn from the top of the great tower by two fans in the basement. The air enters through openings about 250 feet above the street level, and is drawn down through the turrets on the two front corners of the tower as far as the roof, where it passes into two flues, one on either side, each 12 feet by 5, which carry it to the basement.

Here, on each side of the building, it is first drawn through a main coil, containing 9,000 lineal feet of 1-inch pipe, which heat it to 66°F. It is then drawn through washers which clean it from dust and soot and raise its relative humidity by absorption of moisture to about 80 per cent., which will be reduced to about 75 per cent. by further increase of temperature before delivery to the rooms; in the coldest weather the relative humidity will be kept below 50 per cent. to avoid heavy deposits of moisture on the windows. . . . [From the basement the purified air was to be distributed to the various rooms by ductwork.]

[The two towers at the rear of the courtyard were also to be part of the system.] *All of the outlet flues discharge into a main duct in the roof; two rotary fans, similar to those used for the fresh air supply, draw the foul air from the main duct into the two rear towers, by which it is discharged through openings 160 feet above the street level. . . .*

[Regarding the exterior, Richardson says:] *A free treatment of Romanesque has been followed, throughout, as a style especially adapted to the requirements of a large civic building; for while it maintains great dignity together with a strong sense of solidity, it lends itself at the same time most readily to the requirements to utility, especially in the matter of light. To strengthen this feeling of dignity and to express the civic character of the building, the pavilions have been emphasized, and a monumental treatment followed throughout.*

MATERIAL AND DECORATION*. Except in the court yard, where brick is used for the most part* [this, as we have seen, was changed], *the outer walls are all of granite backed with brick. The jambs, mouldings, etc., are of cut stone; otherwise the granite is laid with rock face. In an atmosphere like that of Pittsburgh some accumulation of soot must in any case take place; but the risk of disfigurement from such accumulation and from subsequent washing is reduced to a minimum by altogether avoiding projecting courses, belts and cornices, by introducing carving very sparingly—the decorative work being little more than ordinary good stone cutting—by using only such mouldings as offer the smallest resting place for soot, and by admitting crockets and other projecting members only when protected by overhanging water tables. It will be seen, however, from the accompanying sketches of capitals and moulding profiles, that the result of the treatment proposed will be by no means ineffective.*

The large use of quarry faced stone, the lack of carving, and the absence of projecting courses, belts and cornices, while maintaining and strengthening the dignity of the building, make the stonework extremely economical. . . .

[Regarding the Jail, Richardson says:] The Jail *is joined to the Court House by a covered stone bridge, carried across Ross Street on a single segmental arch, the keystone of which is 26 feet above the level of the street. By this bridge and passages in the Jail and Court House at either end, prisoners may be brought directly from their cells to the rooms of the Criminal Court under shelter and privately, without traversing any public hall, staircase, or ante-room. The relative advantages of a bridge and a tunnel have been carefully considered, and the bridge is preferred as the more economical in construction, as more readily ventilated and lighted, and as affording more direct communication.*

The general plan of the Jail is in the form of an irregular cross: in the shortest arm, fronting on Ross Street, is the main entrance, with the general office and the officers' and witness rooms; the cells fill the three longer arms, and the octagonal guard room occupies the space at the intersection. An L shaped wing occupying all of the space on Ross Street, north of the main entrance, contains the kitchens, laundry and store rooms, and the hospital. A similar wing on the south, extending from the main entrance to Diamond Street, is occupied by the sheriff's house. . . .

The Ross Street front of the Court House in the competition design. The dormers are flush with the walls, and balustrades run between them.

In the design of the exterior, a treatment has been followed similar to that of the Court House, but more severe. Here, as in the Court House, the intention has been to express in the exterior the character and purpose of the interior, and to rely for architectural effect upon the arrangement of the masses, and the dignity and solidity of the construction. The higher walls of the western wing in the centre of the Ross Street front emphasize the position of the main entrance, and the whole front is lightened and given interest by the gables of the hospital and sheriff's house, and by the tower which serves as abutment to the bridge; while the roof lines of the three wings which contain the cells are broken by the ventilating turrets, and by the octagonal lantern of the guard room, which forms the central feature of the whole design.

Respectfully submitted,

H. H. RICHARDSON
Architect

On January 25, the *Chronicle Telegraph* reported:

Four weeks after four architects submitted their plans for the new Court House and Jail, Mr. Richardson. . . was the man whose plans were chosen by a majority of the County Commissioners. The advantages of his plan are superior for lighting and ventilation, a more substantial building and the absence of ''belt courses.'' The general structure of the building was the best suited for a city like Pittsburgh of all those submitted. . . . With these advantages in his favor, he also entered with his plans an offer by an eastern contractor to build at his estimated price of $1,900,000. This was the lowest price suggested by any of the architects. . . . It is proposed to have an architect selected by the first of February. [Apparently the reporter was ''jumping the gun'' in implying that the Commissioners had ''chosen'' Richardson officially.] *The clearing of the portion of the old Court House and Jail now on the lot will be left to the newly assigned architect entirely.*

On January 25, 1884, the Commissioners' *Minutes* noted that a telegram was sent to the architects asking for the terms on which they would perform final architectural work if the Board should accept their plans, and on January 31, ''the Board of County Commissioners present Mercer, McKee and McWilliams with County Engineer Charles Davis, this day selected H. H. Richardson of Brookline, Massachusetts as the supervising architect of the proposed new Court House and Jail.''

The term ''supervising architect,'' which might seem rather ambiguous, was further explained by a statement of Commissioner McKee published in the *Commercial Gazette* for February 1:

We have selected Mr. Richardson because he seemed to have the best ideas of what we wanted and his plans have more good points about them, things we think desirable, I mean, than any of the others. We have not adopted his plans, however, but he will now proceed to make plans carrying out our ideas more fully. Mr. Richardson is a man of very large experience and has a national reputation. There can be no doubt of his competency to render satisfaction.

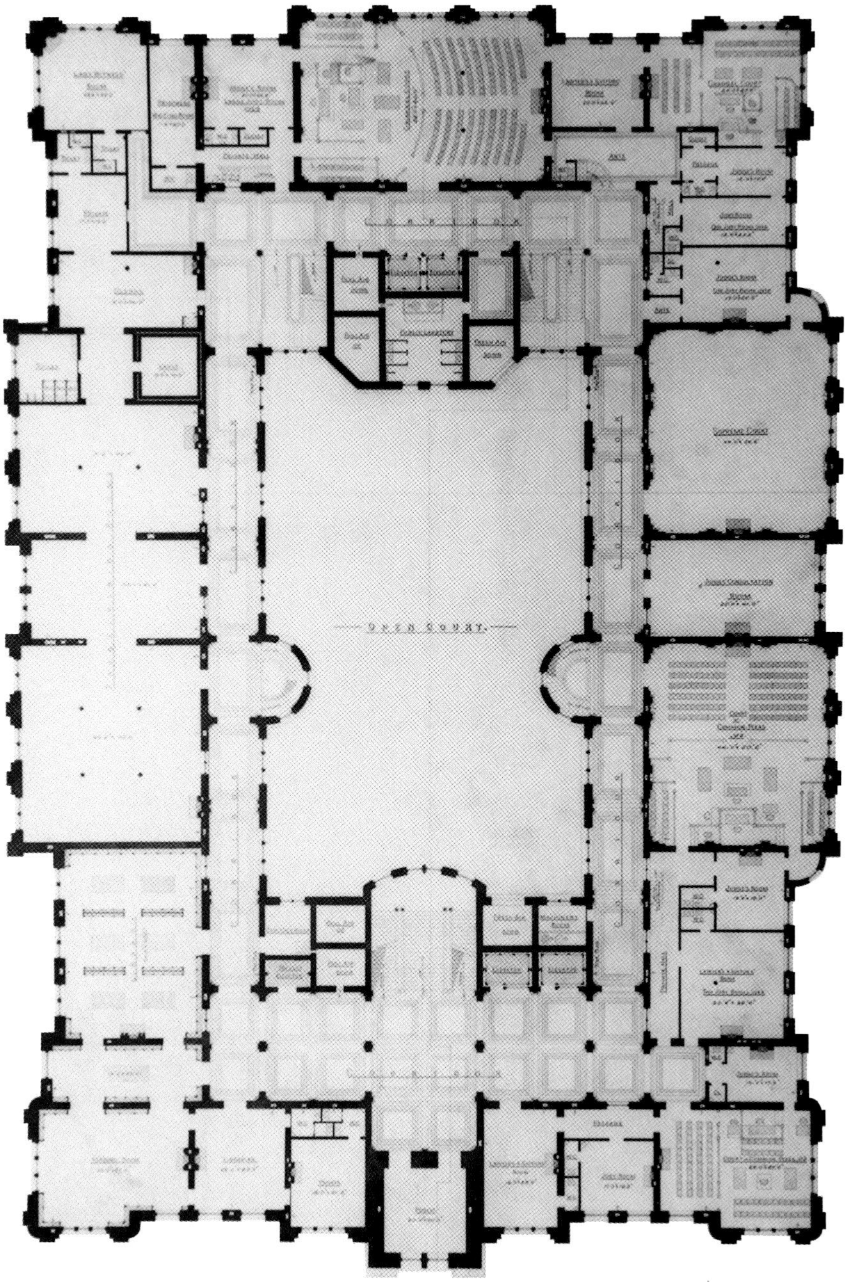

Courtroom floor plans contrasted. William W. Boyington's plan (left) lacks the neatness of Richardson's (right).

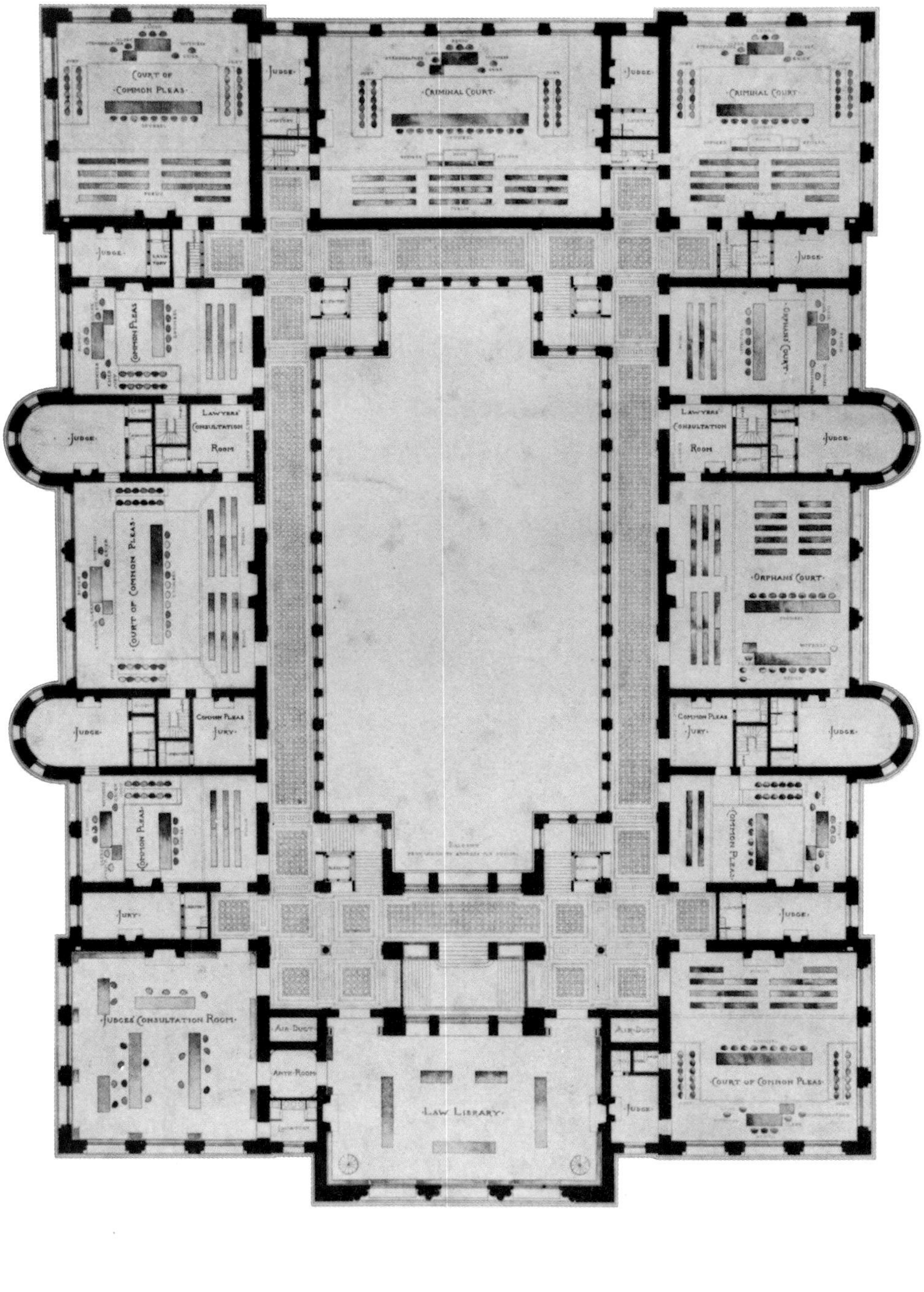
Court of
Common Pleas
Judge
Criminal Court
Judge
Criminal Court
Judge
Judge
Common Pleas
Orphans' Court
Judge
Lawyers' Consultation Room
Lawyers' Consultation Room
Judge
Court of Common Pleas
Orphans' Court
Judge
Common Pleas Jury
Common Pleas Jury
Judge
Common Pleas
Common Pleas
Jury
Judge
Judges' Consultation Room
Air-Duct
Air-Duct
Ante-Room
Law Library
Judge
Court of Common Pleas

On March 15, 1884, the *Commercial Gazette* reported, "Yesterday the County Commissioners and Mr. H. H. Richardson met, and for the last time, considered the contract for the erection of the new county buildings. The conference ended in Messrs. Mercer, McWilliams, and McKee signing on behalf of the County and Mr. Richardson accepted the work."

A historical account, *History of the Erection of the Court House* (Pittsburgh, 1889), by Charles H. McKee, which contains the best abridged version of the contract, says that "Mr. Richardson. . .agreed to furnish and supply on or before July 1st, 1884, all plans, designs and specifications for the proper letting of a contract for the erection of a new Court House and Jail which when fully completed with all necessary appurtenances should not involve a cost exceeding $2,250,000."

When the details of the contract were announced in the public press, there was grumbling at the magnitude of the sum needed to complete the County Buildings, and particularly at the architect's five-percent fee. On March 1, 1884 the *Commercial Gazette* editorialized:

> *In the eyes of the public, $100,000 is a big sum to be given to any one man for a few years individual labor. . . . Two of the leading architects of this city were visited and asked if they thought the Boston man's fee was too large. They replied that five percent is the fee adopted by the American Institute of Architects all over the country and that organization includes most of the eminent men of the profession. In view of this the architects interviewed did not regard the price allowed Mr. Richardson as excessive.*

In connection with the local controversy over the Richardsonian fee, another interview with a Pittsburgh architect, published in the *Evening Penny Press* of August 14, 1884, adds an interesting sidelight on the state of the architectural profession in the city:

> *"None of the architects in this city are getting rich," said a leading member of the profession this morning. "Rates are too low, expenses too heavy, and too many builders work without plans. In the east an architect regularly gets five percent of the cost of his building. In Pittsburgh the rate is three percent, and there are men who are ready to cut even that."*
>
> *"Does anyone make $10,000 a year?"*
>
> *"Oh, no," exclaimed the architect, "To do that he would have to get full rates on $500,000 worth of buildings. . . . I don't think there are four architects in the city who clear half of $10,000. All we can do is make a comfortable living. The only man I knew to get five percent was Kerr, who put up the City Hall, and oh, what a fuss was raised about that! Richardson will do as well with the Court House."*

The Commissioners apparently paid little heed to this local carping, and Richardson was too busy to notice. McKee continues:

From the time the contract was signed Mr. Richardson was feverishly anxious to have the building completed and went at the work with increased energy. He at once increased his corps of skilled assistants to about thirty in number, and had his offices enlarged for their accommodation. Arrangements were made to serve their meals in a dining room adjoining the offices, and with his aides he worked day and night in preparing and perfecting plans for letting of the contract for building.

On July 1, the *Evening Penny Press* reported, "The old Criminal Court room will not be used after today for court purposes, as the County Commissioners intend using it to exhibit plans for construction purposes in connection with the new Court House."

On the preceding day the same paper had announced that "Architect Richardson is expected to arrive here this afternoon from Boston, Massachusetts, with the plans and specifications for the new Court House and Jail complete."

Hetherington's description of design revisions that followed deserves extensive quotation:

Once Richardson had received the commission in 1884, he set about preparing the working plans, in which he changed some aspects of his competition project. Van Rensselaer relates that this was his common practice, to alter his designs occasionally throughout a building's history, from the initial idea to the final construction, thus demonstrating his openness "to fresh inspiration." The most pronounced modification was to place the tower at the front of the courthouse, instead of in the courtyard. In the competition designs, Richardson interpreted the tower behind the front gable in a manner comparable to the four small towers. The grand stairway rose within the lower parts of the clock tower much as the corner towers of the courtyard contained the four secondary stairways and elevators. With the central mass moved forward, Richardson changed his interpretation and was able to open up the main stairway as is mentioned later. On the exterior, the architect effectively removed the abrupt transition from the broad, relatively horizontal mass of the building to its elongated tower.

The people of Allegheny County may have requested the variation after having seen the projects of Ord and Myers, at least, who had clock towers immediately above the main entrances. Perhaps also Boyington, [as in] *his Board of Trade Building, planned to have a tower similarly located* [we do not know that he did]. *Richardson himself may have appreciated this aspect of the other proposals and asked the Commissioners to accept his modified project. In either case, it seems likely that the architect had thought of the new arrange-*

Grant and Diamond Street elevations (top, bottom) in the competition design.

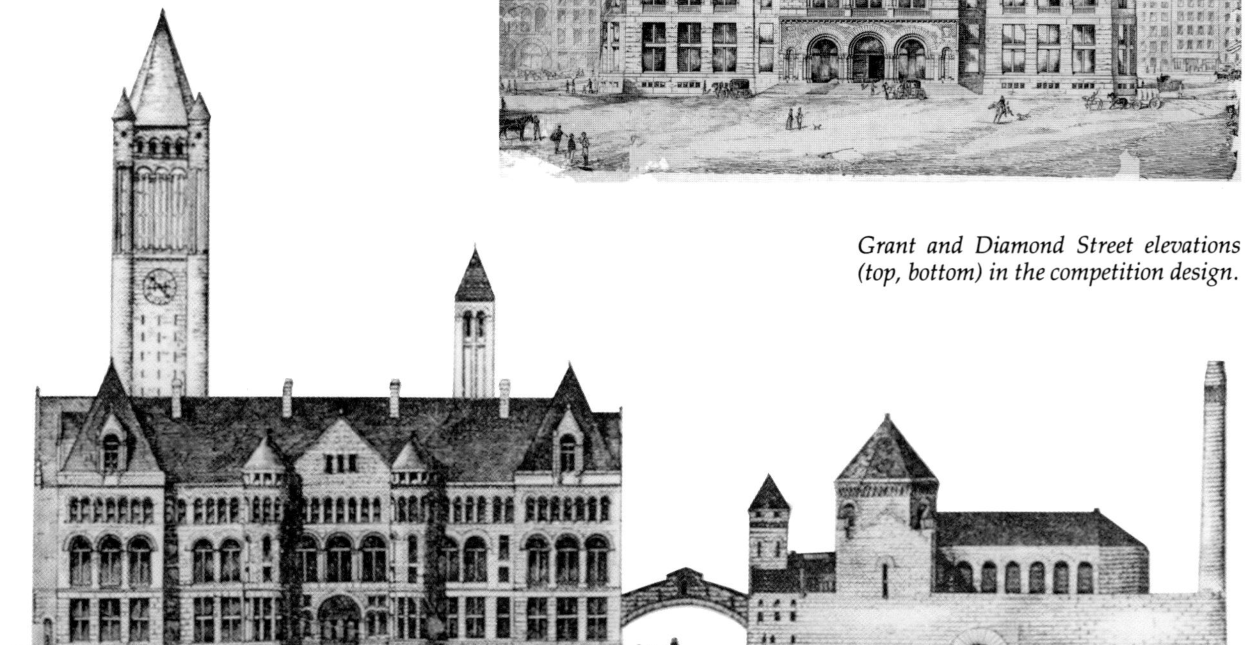

ment in the earliest stages of his designs. To the left of a rough sketch for the Ross Street end of the first floor appears a small doodle of the front elevation with the tower over three wide entrances. This small sketch is remarkably close to the final execution. Another drawing of the Grant Street elevation shows how Richardson was investigating the final modification. The crisp outline of the composition and the sureness with which the fenestration of the pavilions and details of the tower are described would date this drawing from immediately after the competition. Before modifying the appearance of the tower, Richardson moved it directly forward to analyze how it would relate to the whole facade and to a single arched entrance. . . .

Richardson and his office made several studies of the tower. An early one depicts the clock placed within a single arched belfry surrounded by elaborate carving. After the competition, the architect removed the clock and transformed the tower into a slightly more slender shape. The corner turrets are the major support of the tower, and Richardson added four other semi-circular buttresses to his final plans. Those on the north and south sides are placed on square bases and rise to about two-thirds the height of the tower shaft. The other two are smaller, positioned on the front and back of the tower as enlarged piers for a blind arcade that encompasses two rows of slit windows for the storerooms.

The Court House tower rising from Grant Street.

The tower itself seems to "grow" out of its base, through the front roof of the courthouse. Indeed, Richardson has insisted upon this organic quality in moving the tower forward. An early sketch of the tower's base shows how the architect envisioned the massive front element around a central doorway, almost as a tree trunk from which springs the narrow shaft. Henry-Russell Hitchcock [in his monograph on Richardson] *criticizes the architect for having made the Grant Street facade too heavy by moving the tower, and prefers the former design. This is true, in that the library windows lose some of their expressive quality and that the small third story windows provide less light to the tower room than the flanking windows. But the abrupt shift from the original front gable to the seemingly unrelated tower above and behind has been removed. Instead, the solid mass of the tower now relates organically to its base and to the arched entrances with their heavy abutments. Furthermore, the low, tile roof emphasizes the bold height and silhouette of the granite tower. The heaviness of the lower portions and the severity of the shaft contrast successfully with the openness of the tall belfry. Functional as a "snorkel" for ventilation and as storage space, the tower in its new position becomes a more imposing feature than before. It asserts the civic authority of the courthouse and, in the late nineteenth century, it commanded an impressive view onto the city below.*

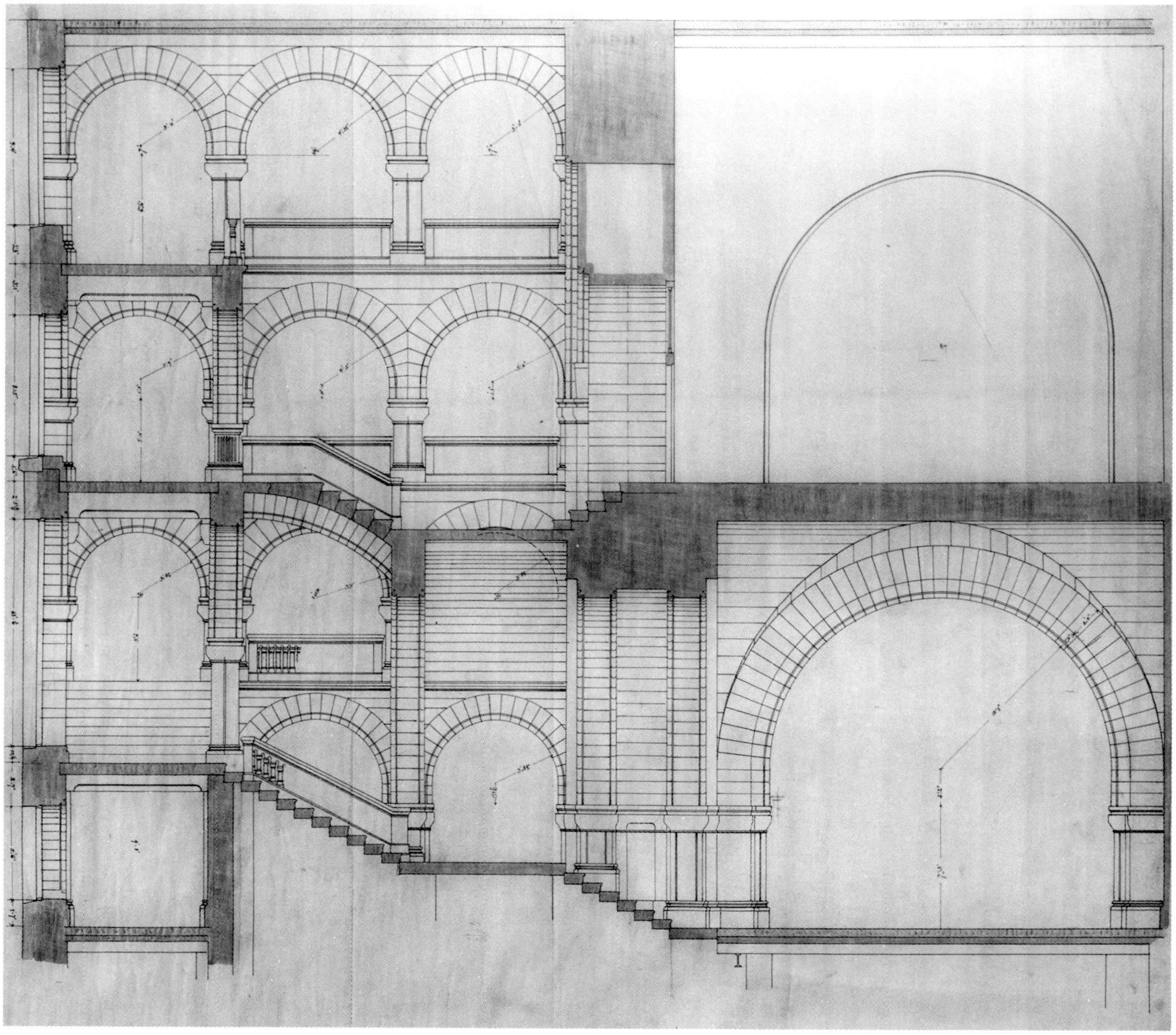

Section through the grand staircase of the Court House as built. The windows to the courtyard are to the left, and the tower rises above the broad spaces on the right.

THE PHOENIX TOWER

THE STORY OF ITS BUILDING JULY-DECEMBER 1884, AND 1885

The Commissioners' *Minutes* note that on June 24, 1884,

the Commissioners resolved that the County Controller bė directed to advertise in one of the leading daily papers of the following cities: Boston, New York, Philadelphia and Chicago, for a period of three consecutive weeks. The advertisement asking for sealed proposals for the erection of a new Court House and Jail at Pittsburgh, Allegheny County, Pennsylvania, will be received at this office by the Commissioners of said County until 2 o'clock A.M. of August 16, 1884.

All proposals must be in accordance with plans and specifications prepared by H. H. Richardson, architect, which will be open for examination at the office of the said County Commissioners on and after the first Monday of July next.

On August 5, the *Evening Penny Press* announced that "architect Richardson is in the city to consult with the County Commissioners relative to the estimates of the contractors. About 40 men are engaged upon bids which will open on the 16th." The *Commercial Gazette* of August 8 also reported that

the old criminal court room is the scene of much hard work now. Broad high tables are stretched across its breadth and in numbers to completely fill the room. On these, on smaller tables crowded into corners, hanging on the walls and lying in every possible nook and corner are the plans for the new Court House. Men in shirt sleeves, armed with foot rules and compasses and huge memorandum books crowd the room. There is no noise, but a great deal of hard work there. The time for making the estimates is shortening rapidly and the architects and contractors are working hard. Among those present are many from other cities. The majority, however, represent contractors of this city.

The *Commercial Gazette* on August 21 again interviewed Richardson and asked him if he anticipated any large additions to the expense of the building before it was completed. He replied, "If this were the last building I expected to handle there might be some object in making it cost as much as possible, but as I expect to continue in the business it is my interest to bring the cost as near the contract as possible. I don't want to ruin my reputation."

The McKee history says:

> *The bids are remarkably close in amount and no little time was required for their consideration in detail. . . . After comparison it was determined that the bid for the erection of the buildings by Norcross Bros. in Worcester granite was the lowest.*
>
> *It should be noticed, especially by those who honestly apprehended that the Commissioners erred in selecting granite because of its being costly, if not extravagant, that it was secured for less money than they could have secured any of the other materials named, and the parties who made the bids for the materials above named, other than granite, afterwards avowed that they could not have erected the buildings in brick for the price named by Norcross Bros. for granite. . . .*
>
> *Then it was that the opposition to the course of the Commissioners grew more determined. Prominent citizens addressed communications urging them to abandon their course. "Solemn protests" in writing were filed "against the contemplated extravagant expenditure of the people's money," "the materials," "the extravagant rate of compensation to be paid to the architect and above all the enormous amount of money intended to be spent in the erection of the buildings." Another objected to "a costly pile of granite unsuitable for the purposes required and in no way in keeping with the good taste and practical common sense of our citizens," and against "jaunting over the country in search of costly model buildings to imitate or copy after, or hunting up and importing costly architects to superintend the work."*

On August 27, 1884, the *Commercial Gazette* said that "nothing had been done toward letting the contract. Ex-judge Thomas Mellon has addressed a letter to the Commissioners objecting on behalf of the taxpayers to their preceeding with the work [mainly on practical but partly on aesthetic grounds]."

> *He. . . objected that "brick would be superior to granite both in beauty and strength. . . . As to the remarkable square tower rising one hundred and fifty feet or more above the roof of the Court House, it strikes me and others, as like a fine building with a grain elevator erected upon it. No one could imagine until he is told, what it is for. . . . As to court rooms, rooms about forty feet square would be the*

right thing and best serve the purposes of justice. The general public have no necessary occasion to be there. . . . There is no need of lobby space for loafers and hangers on."

Despite the objections of the uneasy group of taxpayers whose spokeman was the highly-respected ex-judge Mellon, the Commissioners adhered to their course. On September 1, 1884, the contract for the erection of the Court House and Jail, the exterior walls to be of Worcester granite, was awarded to Norcross Brothers of Worcester, Massachusetts for the sum of $2,243,024.

While the contract was being prepared, the opposition undertook by legal process to restrain the Commissioners. Among other allegations the plaintiffs argued that the debt proposed to be incurred would exceed the amount allowed by law without having first obtained the assent of the electors of the County and that such assent had not been obtained. The plaintiffs prayed that the defendants be enjoined from entering into the proposed contract, and further that they be required to prepare plans and specifications for suitable buildings, such as could be erected without imposing oppressive burdens upon the taxpayers or exceeding the constitutional limits of indebtedness.

The bill was served upon each of the Commissioners on September 10, 1884, and within one hour they met with Norcross Brothers and signed the contract for the erection of the buildings. The Jail was to be finished to the satisfaction of the Commissioners and the architect on or before May 10, 1886, and the basement of the Court House under that part of the office floor intended for the use of the Prothonotary, Register, and Clerk of the Courts was to be ready for occupation on September 1, 1887. The Court House was to be completed and ready for occupation by May 10, 1888.

Norcross Brothers proceeded to tear down the jail and portions of the old Court House that remained and the buildings standing upon the new jail lot.

The McKee history says, however, that

for political purposes the opposition to the Commissioners was kept alive until after the fall election. Some of the newspapers did their utmost to keep it fermented. They made the course of the Commissioners their prominent theme for sensational articles. By cartoons and personal sketches they endeavored to hold members of the board up to ridicule. Blocks of stone were exhibited in a public place, which it was alleged, were procured from the granite quarries at Worcester, from which it was understood that the material for the outer walls was to be brought. As these blocks of stone had little the appearance of red granite, they well answered the purpose in helping to assure the voters of the County that the material selected was wholly unfit for use.

The Commissioners, despite all opposition, were re-elected, and were sufficiently sure of themselves in the meantime to continue as if nothing so important were impending. On October 1, 1884, the *Evening Penny Press* said that

> *the County Commissioners are moving today from the Welsh Church to their office in the new temporary building on Diamond Street, which is now ready for their use... the church building will then be torn down so that the excavating for the new jail foundations now progressing rapidly may proceed without interruption or delay.*

On October 6, the workmen employed by the Pittsburgh construction firm Booth and Flinn to excavate for the foundations of the new Jail struck for higher wages. They were being paid $1.25 per day and decided to ask for $1.50. A fight ensued, and one striker was hit on the head with a brick. When the fight was at its height, the police arrived and arrested all concerned. The strike was settled on October 9, but the rate was still $1.25. Times have changed.

McKee continues the narrative:

> *The complainants* [had meanwhile] *carried the case to the Supreme Court, by which* [a] *decree of the lower court* [favoring the Commissioners] *was affirmed and the appeal dismissed in January, 1886. The expense of the case to the County was over $2,000, but it was the only suit ever brought in relation to the construction of the buildings in which the County was in any way concerned.*
>
> *Most of the plaintiffs afterward conceded their error. Doubtless most of them were actuated in their course by proper and commendable motives, but that some of them were not was shown by their subsequent conduct.*
>
> *The work of erecting the structures proceeded quietly and steadily. The builders continued with their work regardless of the equity proceedings which were pending and in 1884 completed the foundations of the Jail and also made preparations for the laying of the foundations for the Court House.*
>
> *During the year 1885 the work was mostly confined to the erection of the Jail. In making ready for the foundations of the Court House over 80,000 cubic yards of earth were removed, much of which was good brick clay, and was hauled to a brick yard, moulded and burned into bricks, which were brought back and built into the interior walls of the building.*
>
> *As the excavations increased in depth the material grew harder until solid rock was reached, which was blasted out with dynamite and the foundations of both buildings were in all parts laid upon a natural foundation of solid rock. Upon the rock was placed a bed of cement and upon this were laid large blocks of sandstone.*

The Court House and Jail as built.

In February 1885 the drawings for the County Buildings were published for the first time in a large national general-circulation magazine, *Harper's Weekly*. This was probably done at the behest of the noted architectural critic Montgomery Schuyler (1843-1914), who was editor of the magazine from 1885 to 1887. The anonymous description accompanying the drawings does not seem to have been written by Schuyler, but it is interesting as evidence of the degree to which the buildings had already attracted national notice:

The buildings which Mr. H. H. Richardson has designed for Pittsburgh are noteworthy for size, massiveness, and costliness even among the civic palaces of the last decade in this country. They comprise a Court-house and Jail. The Court-house is about half the size of the new Capitol in Albany. . . . The towers serve. . . practical as well as picturesque purposes. Two of them, in the court, rise 75 feet above the ridge of the roof, while the main tower, in the centre of the principal front, attains the unusual height of 318 feet, sixty feet more, if we remember aright, than Trinity spire in New York. The other building is a jail, actually and architecturally united with the Court-house by a "Bridge of Sighs," and built of the same material—a granite, used rock-faced in the fields of wall, and dressed in the belting courses, arches, and cornices. The total cost is to be not far from two millions. . . .

The chief interest of the work will not be in its size and cost, but in its ingenious and in some points novel planning, and in its bold and effective architecture. Both the planning and the architecture are modified to meet the pecular local requirements of Pittsburgh, the chief peculiarity of the local requirements being that the building shall be continually swathed in coal smoke. As fine a site as the city affords has been secured for the new buildings, but no site which is convenient for the transaction of the public business is free from the plague of smoke. In planning a public building for Pittsburgh, therefore, it is necessary that special provision should be made both for lighting and ventilation. Every room in the Pittsburgh Court-house is directly lighted either from the street or from the court, while the principal rooms receive light from both. This is managed by putting the corridors which form the circulatory system of the building on the inner side surrounding the court, and giving them only half the height of the principal rooms, leaving above their ceilings a space which is pierced with windows giving light to the principal rooms, and forming galleries in the first story, while in the second, the corridors being roofed over, the windows above it open directly into the courtrooms.

The system of ventilation is still more peculiar. The main tower rises "above the smoke and stir of this dim spot which men call" Pittsburgh, and the supply of air is to be drawn from this upper level beyond the smoke strata through openings in the turrets 250 feet from the sidewalk. . . . This arrangement exists as yet, of course, only on paper, but is evident to whoever has sojourned in Pittsburgh that some very special provision is needful to make its soot either transparent or respirable.

The architecture is modified to the atmosphere mainly by the reduction to a minimum of the projected points or belts which invite the lodgement of soot. . . . The contrast of rough granite and richly wrought dark sandstone, which is so effective in many of his works, notably in Trinity Church in Boston and in the Albany City Hall, is abandoned here, possibly in favor of a more assured durability than sandstone promises. . . . The use of monochrome, and especially of the pale monochrome of granite, makes it especially difficult to give force to the main features of composition. The architect has undertaken to overcome this difficulty in the present case of increasing the size of the important members, so as to effect by magnitude what he is prohibited from doing by contrast of color or by sharpness and elaboration of modelling. The huge voussoirs of the triple portal at the principal entrance, and of the openings above it, are sure to "tell" even in the smoky air of Pittsburgh, and were they even simpler than they are in modelling. Nevertheless, it is perhaps fortunate that the efforts of the architect to avoid soot can not be so completely successful as to prevent the construction from being occasionally accented by the atmosphere. Whether that happens or not, the principal front

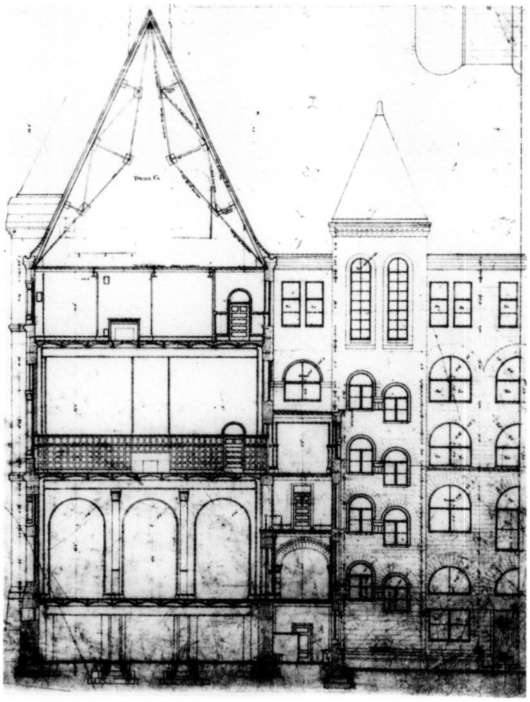

Section through the Ross Street front of the Court House as built, with the courtyard to the right.

Pittsburgh smoke around 1880, rising from the industrial plants of the Monongahela River shore. To the right are the spires of St. Paul's Cathedral and the second Court House designed by John Chislett.

> *of the Pittsburgh Court-house, with its massive tower visible to the bottom, will be one of the boldest and most effective architectural compositions to be seen in this country.*

The *Harper's Weekly* author was preoccupied with practical matters—the ventilation system and the effect of the smoke-laden atmosphere of Pittsburgh on the exterior walls—but also was aware of the grandeur of Richardson's design.

It is interesting that at this same time—perhaps due to the *Harper's Weekly* article—Richardson was asked by the County Commissioners of Butler County to design a new Court House in Hamilton, Ohio. The *Minutes* of the Butler County Commissioners of March 12, 1885 show the following notations:

> *Motion #2... that seven architects be named by the Board and be requested to present floor plans and elevations for the new Court House in competition. The Court House to be built of Berea stone* [sandstone] *first class in quality, to have slate roof, tile floor, and to be a fireproof building throughout, and to have ample accommodations for all County offices... to cost not more than $175,000.*

Among the architects named were "E. E. Meyers" (sic) of Detroit and H. H. Richardson of Boston. The rest were local Ohio men. On March 30, the *Minutes* record "that Meyers [sic], D. W. Gibbs and Company [of Toledo, Ohio] and Richardson be invited to prepare and present complete plans, specifications, and detail drawings and that they be paid a reasonable compensation for said services." At this point the original motion was withdrawn and changed to a motion that Gibbs be appointed architect of the Court House. So far as is known none of the Richardson competition sketches have survived in the Hamilton archives. It is interesting to consider, however, that there might have been a Richardson pendant to the Allegheny County Buildings in Ohio.

McKee continues the history of the Pittsburgh Court House:

> *The 13th day of October, 1885, was the forty-ninth anniversary of the laying of the corner stone of the former Court House, and on that day, the corner stone of the new Court House was laid. It was an immense block of granite, and was laid without conventional ceremonies at the north east corner of the building. When it was prepared and arrangements completed for its being laid, notice was given to the Commissioners. They directed that there be placed under the corner stone, the relics found in the corner stone of the old Court House, together with copies of the contracts relating to the new, a copy of the Bill in Equity, and answer, coins of the day, and other things intended for the information of future ages, about which were folded copies of the daily press, care being taken to include all newspapers*

containing articles relative to the erection of the buildings. The articles were deposited in a box and placed upon the foundation. The corner stone was lowered with a derrick and placed in proper position with its cavity over the box. . . . No stone in the building was laid more quietly.

Now that the foundations were in and the corner stone laid, the walls of Richardson's Court House began to rise.

Construction, c.1885, on the Court House (above) and the Jail (below).

THE PHOENIX TOWER

THE STORY OF ITS BUILDING, 1886-87

According to the Controller's Report issued on January 1, 1886, "the work of erecting the new Court House and Jail has progressed so rapidly that (unless some unforeseen circumstance occurs) the completion of the Jail for occupancy by the time agreed upon, viz:—May 10th, 1886, is no longer questionable."

The lower walls of the Court House were beginning to be visible, and their rise was much assisted by the ingenious construction machinery devised by the contractors. McKee describes it as follows:

First arose within the middle of the square a peculiar frame-work well braced and supported. Around it was attached a system of derricks, composed of masts and horizontal booms, which constituted one of the notable features of the work. In lifting the materials into place on the Court House, ten derricks were used. The mast of each turned upon a steel-pointed pivot and had attached to it a large boom. The masts with their booms were so placed that in their swing the whole area of the Court House was covered within the circles which they inscribed. Upon each boom was laid a track and upon it a carriage with pulleys. Over these a rope was passed, to the end of which was suspended a set of grappling irons. In each case, the other end of the rope led over pulleys and finally to a windlass with which was connected a steam engine. At each of the two engines used stood an engineer who upon being signalled started his engine, which wound or unwound the rope as might be required, to raise or lower the grappling irons. By means of these derricks each piece of material was lifted and conveyed to its exact position. The heavy belt courses, each piece of which weighed tons, were gradually put in place and the service of but a few men were required in handling the most massive materials. In connection with this remarkable system of derricks signals were conveyed over electric wires. Many times over the motive power used was not in sight and to an observer this system of

> *derricks as seen in picking up and carrying materials to place seemed to act as though possessed of intelligence. To the perfection of this arrangement of Messrs. Norcross Brothers was attributable the remarkable rapidity and quickness with which the building progressed.*

It is curious to us nowadays to read of the almost magical effect of these cranes on the sensibility of the nineteenth-century writer. He was capable of wonder when confronted with the new angels and demons of an emerging technology. The man who watched the cranes that acted ''as though possessed of intelligence'' was at a crucial point in our civilization where the observer could look back on the pre-technological past and yet face forward to a future full of mechanical wonders. This was the dual character of the Allegheny County Buildings as well as Richardson. The buildings partake of both the past and the present—they are documents of their times—as did their architect. Here are the efficient, fireproof courtrooms enclosed in the forms and the detailing of the remote medieval past, as well as the erection of the remarkable tower, presided over by electric signals. The County Buildings are transitional documents, not only in themselves but in regard to modern sensibility.

In speaking further of the building of the Court House and Jail, McKee again strikes the note, found throughout his ''history,'' of something dedicated and special inherent in the event. One is asked to contemplate a high and noble enterprise conducted a step beyond the usual range of human condition and therefore slightly supernatural:

> *At no time was the work delayed. . . . Gradually one story rose above another until the third was completed and shortly the red tile roof was made to cover all. . . .*
>
> *During the years in which the work was carried on* [as] *in almost all undertakings requiring the services of a large number of men much difficulty was met by reason of strikes, but neither discord nor contention interrupted or marred the harmony which prevailed amongst the men engaged upon this building, and the work did not at any time cease until its completion.*
>
> *The architect in his office prepared his plans and specifications for each piece of material required. Upon his drawings were shown the exact dimensions of each piece of granite used in the outer walls, a full sized detailed drawing of each piece of cut and ornamental work required, and also drawings showing the exact dimensions of each piece of iron used. Copies of these were supplied to the builders, the superintendent of work, and the County.*
>
> *Each piece of granite in the buildings was fashioned and prepared in the quarries of Worcester, and marked and numbered for its appropriate place in the buildings before being brought to Pittsburgh. In like manner sandstones were prepared and brought from the*

quarries in Beaver Valley, Pennsylvania, for foundations; limestone from Indiana for stairs; marble from Tennessee for wainscoting; Akron tile from Ohio for roofing; and all merged into the building. The beams, trusses, and girders, and all other work in iron, and things in brass, as well as the plate glass used, and tile for the floors were all wrought within the County of Allegheny.

Besides granite and other materials there were used in the construction of the building 157,222 cubic feet of stone for foundation; 96,774 pounds of iron pipe; 230 feet of earthen drain pipe; 11,680 pounds of brass; 14,332,140 bricks; 81,299 hollow bricks; 24,500 enameled bricks; 1,187,136 pounds of rolled iron beams, 54,553 pounds of galvanized iron; 1,308,317 pounds of cast iron; 2,580,909 pounds of wrought iron; 617,119 feet of roof tile; 306 windows; 56,861 yards of plastering; 56,000 yards of white washing; 80 doors; 11,841 feet of slate; 28,197 feet of plate glass; and 38,464 feet of tile for the floor. Electric wires and pipes many miles in length were used, and over 100 miles of copper wire were used in fastening the tiles upon the roof of the Court House alone.

As the solidity of the foundation became apparent and the character of the material became known beyond doubt, words of approval were heard. Day by day, as one course of granite was made to surmount another, expressions of satisfaction were heard on all sides.

In the archives of the Controller's Office there is preserved an undated letter signed by Richardson that proves that the question of furniture for the Court House had been discussed before his death:

I did not understand that any fixed furniture other than mantelpieces, bowls, urinals, sinks, wainscote, was to be provided for by the contract. It is in my opinion very undesirable that any desks, rails, bookcases or other furniture for special uses should be designed until the walls are up, and until those who are to use the rooms can see the spaces to be furnished and give minute directions as to their special wants. If the Commissioners think proper to reserve out of the $2,250,000 the sum of $50,000 for such fixed furniture to be designed by me after the walls are up, I shall not object, and I consider that sum to be a fair allowance for the purpose provided the designs are no more expensive than those I made up for the City Hall at Albany, N.Y., and I think $2,200,000 enough for the building itself.

This letter is again an evidence of Richardson's constant care, his passionate concern with the County Buildings. Aside from that, however, it is final proof that Richardson had nothing to do with the design of the Court House furnishings, since the building was far from finished at the time of his death. The Commissioners did not take his offer to use part of the original contract money because Shepley, Rutan and Coolidge made

Joinery at the Court House: a gate in a courtroom.

up a separate set of specifications for the furnishings in 1888.

And now the passing of Richardson from the scene was not far distant. McKee continues:

> *Long before that remarkable square tower rising one hundred and fifty feet or more above the roof of the Court House had begun to show above the other parts of the building, the beauty, as well as the utility of the structure attracted much attention. By the time that the building was completed to that stage, the architect had completed nearly all his plans to the minutest detail. He was justly proud of his work and took great delight in commenting on it. In speaking of the appreciation in which he would be held, he said, "If they honor me for the pygmy things I have already done, what will they say when they see the Pittsburgh Court House!"*

Mrs. Van Rensselaer also comments on the architect's intense preoccupation with the County buildings:

> *In Richardson's own estimation the Pittsburgh building was the great*

work of his life—the most interesting and important as a problem and the most entirely successful in result. . . . He knew his life might be very short and was almost feverishly anxious to see the Court-house complete before he died. ''Let me have time to finish Pittsburgh,'' he often exclaimed, ''and I should be content without another day.''

''But,'' McKee continues,

his wish to see this the proudest work of his busy and renowned career, was not to be gratified. On the 27th day of April, 1886 he was suddenly called away. No incident during the progress of the work cast such a profound feeling of sorrow over others connected with it, as did his death.

After his body was laid to rest, the same three Commissioners were in office, who at the time of making the contract with him, had personally assured him that in case of his death, his executors should be preferred to all others to take charge of and complete his work. The promise was kept, and the work proceeded to completion under his executors' supervision.

These executors were George Foster Shepley, Charles Hercules Rutan, and Charles Allerton Coolidge, who had constituted themselves as a ''firm'' primarily to finish Richardson's contracted obligations. Besides the Allegheny County buildings there were 24 other projects unfinished. Shepley and Coolidge, who had joined Richardson's staff in the early 1880s, were, together with Rutan, who was Richardson's engineer, the great architect's choice as his successors. Their firm became one of the largest architectural offices in America during the 1890s and the first decade of the twentieth century.

Under their supervision the Court House work went on without any difficulties. The Jail was ready for occupancy in May 1886, although the Commissioners in the interest of the health of the prisoners did not allow it to be occupied until September 1 of that year, ''so that it, being of stone might be thoroughly dried.''

The progress of the construction was ''news'' beyond the city, and in September 1886 the *American Architect* published a drawing of the courtyard of the Court House.

By December, the walls of the Court House were sufficiently completed so that the stone carvers from Evans and Tombs of Boston, who held the contract for the carving, were at work. On December 28, 1886, the *Commercial Gazette* reported that

clinging to the grey granite walls of the new Court House are several shaky platforms, roofed and walled with canvas. In some of these a smoking stove-pipe suggests a human habitation. It is cold weather away up there just now, and that is the way the sculptors engaged in carving the exterior of the handsome window frames and cornices,

Granite at the Court House: an interior column bearing Richardson's monogram, and the Ross Street entrance as it now is.

keep themselves warm. Their tiny stoves do not burn with natural gas, but ordinary laborers carry up coal to them every few hours. The clatter, chiseling and hammering on the outside of the building is very interesting. There are at present 26 carvers employed on different parts of the immense new Court House in beautifying the rough and hard granite into numerous artistic designs compatible with the Byzantine [sic] *style in which the building is to be executed.*

These men of whom 13 are Italians and the rest Americans, are all day long standing on their scaffolds under their canvas roofs plying their tools vigorously into the hard stone. They do their work according to plaster of paris molds which are furnished them by their employers. The business they are engaged in required a great deal of study and practice. They earn from $4 to $6 a day for ten hours work. It is necessary that they should be able to draw and make their own designs on stone, before they use their hammers and chisels. . . .

The men at work are all experienced workmen who have served in their trade for many years. There is an old Italian, Geromo Bargali, who was born in a small village near the great marble quarries of Carrara in Italy. He has been a marble cutter, a sculptor and in fact has gone through a great many adventurous experiences and vicissitudes in his mechanical career. He has worked in all the large cities of Europe such as Vienna, Prague, Munich, Berlin, Stuttgart, Berne, Paris, Rome, and even Madrid, until he gradually drifted into Boston from whence he was sent to this city. The men will have finished the carving of the exterior in about 9 or 10 months.

At the end of 1886, the County Engineer reported:

By terms of contracts for new County Buildings, as well as by Act of Assembly, the County Engineer is required to exercise a supervisory duty in connection with this work.

The work on these buildings has made a very gratifying progress. The Jail was finished in June last, and occupied in September.

The Court House (except tower) is now ready for the roof, and one quarter of the building has roof trusses in place.

The labor strikes, while causing serious delays and derangements in building operations in some quarters, did not materially affect the work here.

The sudden death of the architect H. H. Richardson on the 27th of April last, might have been the cause of a very serious delay in the completion of the buildings, but fortunately he had matured all his plans and completed his working drawings so that his former associates and successors in business were able to take charge and fully carry out his ideas without change or alteration.

On January 5, 1887 the *Commercial Gazette* reported that "Shepley,

Rutan and Coolidge. . . yesterday wrote to the Commissioners for impressions of the State and County seals, which are to be cut in stone and placed on either side of the main entrance to the Court House." In mid-year the architects appointed Charles D. Austin as supervising architect, inasmuch as Frank Alden, supervising architect heretofore, was now well-launched on an architectural career of his own in Pittsburgh.

Later in the year an article appeared in the *Bulletin* on the perennial question of cutting down the Hump. City Engineer Edward Manning Bigelow suggested that Fifth Avenue might be cut down, allowing Grant Street to remain at the present level and constructing a bridge so that it could cross Fifth. The article also states that the new Court House had been constructed with the proposed cut in mind. If so, Richardson had not allowed for such a deep cut as was finally made in 1912.

The year 1887 was rather uneventful for the new Court House; construction went steadily ahead. In the Controller's Report for 1887, County Engineer Charles Davis reported that

> *the Court House is now about finished so far as the constructive work is concerned; all that remains of outside work is the topping out of the stone roof of the tower, and the setting of platforms and steps in front of the building and putting up iron area protection railings on the side walks.*

The State seal on the Grant Street front.

THE PHOENIX TOWER

THE STORY OF ITS BUILDING, 1888

The progress of construction had been so rapid that

the completed Court House and Jail was turned over to the Commissioners in April 1888. The contractors would have completed their contract before the day required, which was in three years and six months from the date of its signing, but the Commissioners delayed the finishing of the tower from October to April by the advice of the architects.

Meanwhile, the Commissioners' *Minutes* under the date of February 1888 record that "Mr. Austin presented plans and specifications of furniture needed for the new Court House. [Shepley, Rutan and Coolidge] shall advertise for bidders until 3 o'clock, March 15,1888." On February 10 and 11, the Commissioners interviewed representatives of the Westinghouse, Brush, Edison, and United States companies in regard to the projected electric light plant. On February 28, the County Commissioners let the contract for installing 69 grates in the Court House.

On March 3, the Pittsburgh *Bulletin* reported that

the placing of the topmost layers on the tower of the new Court House completes the enduring picture in stone which was born in the brain of lamented Richardson. It is the final touch to a grand work that must cause a reform in Pittsburgh architecture. The beauty and dignity of the great buildings dwarfing all the structures in its vicinity cannot fail to arouse a desire for better things in architecture. The new Court House silently but eloquently exerts a potent influence. As a court of justice it tells of the majesty of the law; as a thing of rare beauty in granite it preaches the gospel of better architecture in the Iron City.

Also on March 7, the *Press* featured the Court House with the headline, "The Court House Lions/Beautiful stone figures that guard the entrances":

> *People have been going in numbers this week to take a look at the lions and other things just finished. . . . A stroll through the place today showed persons in almost every room looking in admiration. Some of them had apparently come from country places. From inquiries at the constructor's office it would seem that there is a regular stream of country builders and architects asking every day to be shown over the building. It is a point of business they make in coming to town to take a run up to the Court House before going away.*
>
> *The lions at the gate are couchant* [actually, they are "sejant"] *and are carved from Milford granite. They look ready to spring on anyone who should presume to go into the new temple of justice with an injudicious plea. They are eight feet high, and it took two artificers, three months to execute them.*
>
> *A little controversy is going on among the local stone contractors and builders about the paving around the building that is just being completed. The stone used is Ohio berea. Some say that berea is not durable and should not be used for this purpose; others say that the stone has been tried around the new Jail and other places, and it has held up well. . . although a better material could undoubtedly have been found. . . . Time alone will show.*
>
> *The grand stair-case is now completely visible. . . . The plinths and bases of the vestibule are now being polished, and the Vermont purple slate of which they are made looks very handsome. Several country visitors today had grouped themselves about one of the twelve polished granite pillars and seemed quite dazed with the vista of arches. . . . Finishing touches are now being given to the stone capitals and plinths of the columns. . . . Italian masons have done nearly all the work. One of those at work today said that one foot per day was about the best speed that had been made on the limestone floral capitals.*
>
> *One cannot help but admire, on entering one of the spacious courtrooms, the magnificent oaken dadoes that run around the walls. Such work used to be called wainscoting, but Oscar Wilde knocked that old-fashioned word in the head and the aesthetic world has decreed to hear it no more. The oak panelings are eight feet high. . . and give a satisfaction to the eye in which all people of taste must rejoice.*

In regard to the Court House lions, it is interesting to compare this 1888 opinion with a more modern description taken from an essay I wrote about lion sculpture in Pittsburgh:

> *Possibly the most important, certainly the most elegant and mysterious of this maned host are the two large seated beasts that flank the Grant Street entrance arches of the Court House. It is appropriate that the portals of Justice be so guarded and architecturally these symbols are even more apt because the Court House may be spoken*

A lion by the left-hand doorway on the Grant Street front. Before the Hump was lowered, the steps rose to the bottom of the plinth on which the lion sits. This view illustrates Richardson's detailing, including the ornament that some critics have dismissed as cold and academic.

of as a lion among Pittsburgh buildings. Since the level of Grant Street was lowered after the completion of the building, the statues are rather difficult to see properly, but their lofty position makes them seem even more remote. Of all our carved animals, they are the strangest, the most exotic, and they have the air of not really belonging to the city—of being, rather, distinguished foreign visitors. . . .

It is interesting that [they] *appear to be lions of the Classical Renaissance-Academic tradition done up in Byzantine costume and Milford granite. Whatever their stylistic provenance, how splendid, how subtle are these superbeasts! The curled hieratic animals hunched elegantly backward seem to emerge out of the crisp surface of the rock-faced walls like fairy tale princes from an enchanted wood. Lords of some lost kingdom, imperial* flaneurs, *grand fops, they lower their veiled eyes with an exquisite disdain, a fierce aloof defiance on the commercial (and political) monotonies of the street below.*

On March 19 the furniture bids were opened, and the bid was awarded to Norcross Brothers. On March 24, the *Bulletin* wrote:

> *An Eastern firm built the new Court House and the same firm is going to furnish the splendid building. If the honest methods manifested in the construction of the pile will be continued in the work of furnishing, our people will have no cause for regret, even though Pittsburgh enterprise did not get a chance to show itself in the getting of the furniture contract.*

On April 9 another $100,000 was awarded to Norcross Brothers and $30,000 to Shepley, Rutan and Coolidge, and on April 10, plans, designs, and specifications for chandeliers and interior painting were submitted and approved by Shepley, Rutan, and Coolidge. They were requested to advertise for bids until April 21.

The *Commercial Gazette* reported on June 6 that

> *all windows in the first, second and third stories as well as those of the first and second floor halls will have shades of the best hand painted cloth and will be provided with spring rollers, brackets, and nickel rings,* [and] *will be worked with braided silver cord. The windows in the court rooms on the second story and the Supreme Court Room on the third floor will have curtains made of the best double faced Titian velour, hung from oak poles.*

On April 16, the climactic moment in the construction of the Court House arrived:

> *At two o'clock P.M. the cap stone. . . was placed in position. The day is bright and clear with a cool air blowing from the Northwest. The derrick on the top and the scaffolding was decorated with the American flag and presented a sight seldom seen which caused crowds of citizens to gather at many points to witness the sight.*

On August 10, the Commissioners' *Minutes* recorded the following:

> *Whereas H. H. Richardson, architect and designer of the new Court House died before its completion, and whereas many of his friends and admirers, citizens of Allegheny County, have requested that an inscription to his memory be placed in a suitable location on the Grand Stairway in the new Court House. Therefore be it resolved that the following inscription as presented by his friends and admirers of this County, to wit:*
>
> *"In memory of Henry Hobson Richardson, Architect, 1838-1886—Genius and training made him master of his profession. Although he died in the prime of life, he left to his country many monuments of art, foremost among them this temple of Justice."*
>
> *be adopted as presented and the Architects be instructed to have*

The entrance to the law library through the rear wall of the tower. The impost blocks carry the memorial inscription to Henry Hobson Richardson.

the same inscribed on the capstone [i.e., the impost blocks] *at the right and left sides of the main entrance to the Law Library.*

It was accordingly done, and the inscription still presides magnificently at the top of the great staircase. If anything more were needed to testify to the esteem in which Richardson was held by the citizens of Allegheny County, these words would be sufficient. Thereby the building was dedicated to the architect and the whole structure became his monument.

On August 16, the *Press* reported that ''Percy Digby supervised the moving of the law library to the new Court House. Twelve men were employed to move 16,000 volumes. The new quarters are at the Grant Street front under the big tower.''

The *Commerical Gazette* recorded on September 1:

The September term of court will open on Monday in the new Court House; Judge Ewing presiding in Criminal Court. The Sheriff's office will be moved to their new quarters today. The Clerk of Courts moved yesterday and the only remaining occupants of the old building are the Controller, Treasurer and the County Commissioners who expect to move all together in a day or two.

Ross Street looking toward Fifth Avenue, around 1910.

On September 3 the same paper reported the opening of the Bridge of Sighs:

> *That unique and very elegant piece of architecture that connects the Jail with the new Court House will be inaugurated today. The occasion, unlike that of the opening of other bridges will not be one of joy and festivity, but on the contrary will be a sad one, as many of those who will take part in the ceremony will do so ''betwixt hope and fear,'' since it is to be used solely for conveying prisoners to and from Criminal Court. Prisoners speculate as to what extent their being first to cross the bridge will affect their sentences. Once the prisoners had to be guarded and handcuffed, but no more, because the bridge makes escape impossible.*

If the prisoners were betwixt hope and fear, Charles McKee used another conception of ''betweenness'' in his history of the building of the Court House: ''The Court House and the Jail being connected by a bridge, destined to become famous, the observation 'a palace and a prison on each hand' was often used as peculiarly appropriate.''

The *Commercial Gazette,* on September 3, recorded:

> *The elegant court rooms in the new public building are now ready for occupancy and the September term of Quarter Sessions will open today in the new quarters. It must be a matter of infinite pride and satisfaction to every taxpayer as he looks upon this massive structure to reflect that it has been brought through all its various stages to entire completion without waste and extravagance on the one hand or parsimony on the other. No taint of corruption or suspicion of jobbery attaches to anyone in connection with the work, and the people have the satisfaction of knowing that every dollar of their money has been honestly expended.*

On September 7, the *Pittsburgh Press* reported that plans for the observance of the Centennial of Allegheny County were under way. The Court House was to be formally dedicated on Monday, September 24, 1888, and a grandstand was to be set up at the main entrance.

The *Commercial Gazette* reported on September 22 that ''yesterday work on decorating the exterior of the Court House for the Dedication Exercises began in earnest, under the direction of Frank I. Cooper. The decorations are to cost $1,500.''

So the stage was prepared for the formal ceremonies signifying that the Court House was completed and ready for its public career in the city of Pittsburgh.

Opposite: view north along Ross Street, with the Bridge of Sighs, around 1900. The old Western University of Pennsylvania building is at the far left.

THE TOWER DEDICATED

AN INTERLUDE

The dedication exercises marked the official acceptance and celebration of the new County Buildings. A handsome engraving of Richardson's Court House was on the cover of the Official Program. The program contained a description of the Centennial celebration events:

> *On the morning of the Centennial Anniversary of the existence of the County of Allegheny, a large assemblage of citizens congregated in front of the new Court House, for the purpose of its dedication.*
>
> *The exercises were conducted upon a platform, in front of the building, on which were accomodated the speakers, the music, county officials, and twenty-five hundred citizens of the county. Thousands were gathered in front of and near to this platform.*
>
> *Promptly at ten o'clock ''Hail Columbia'' was rendered by the Centennial Orchestra, after which the meeting was called to order by Hon. Morrison Foster, Chairman of the Centennial Committee, who said:*
>
> *''People of Allegheny County: As Chairman of the Centennial Committee, I have the honor to call this meeting to order. You will be kind enough to preserve perfect order and quiet. You are assembled here today as the owners of this vast pile, this beautiful piece of architecture—the finest in America—to receive it from the hands of the County Commissioners, and to dedicate it to public use.* [Applause.] *You are here as the owners of this magnificent temple of justice, in the dedication of which we will now commence our Centennial exercises.* [Applause.]

The meeting was formally opened with prayer by the Rev. R. H. Coster. The Centennial Orchestra then played ''The Star Spangled Banner''; this was followed by the presentation of the Court House to the people of Allegheny County by Robert E. Mercer, president of the Board of County Commissioners. Mr. Mercer then spoke. The buildings were received on behalf of the people by William McCullough Darlington. ''The Red, White and Blue'' was played by the Centennial Orchestra. The history of the erection of the Court House prepared and submitted by Charles H. McKee was then accepted by the officials and made part of the record.

Next in order was the address of the Honorable J. W. F. White, who among other things said:

In every mind present two thoughts are struggling for utterance—first, the marvelous growth of our county, and second, the grandeur of this temple of justice. Both are subjects of profound gratification.

Excluding from consideration the eight northern counties, carved out of the original territory, in 1800, we confine our view to Allegheny County with its present boundaries. Starting with a population of less than 6,000, it now approaches 500,000, a greater population than in either of eight separate States of the Federal Union, including three of the original thirteen. Pittsburgh, in 1788, had 500 inhabitants; it now has over 300,000. I count Allegheny and the adjoining boroughs and districts parts of Pittsburgh. By contiguity, business relations and community of interests they are all essentially and logically parts of the city, and should be embraced in one municipal government. Pittsburgh would then take its proper stand among cities, and be ranked in the census table as the eighth city in the United States, instead of the twelfth, as now.

One hundred years ago Allegheny County had not one manufacturing establishment. Now it is one of the great manufacturing centres of the world. There is more capital invested in manufactories in this county alone, than in either of twenty-six different States of the Union, including seven of the original thirteen, and the value of the annual products far greater than in any one of the twenty-six.

Wonderful indeed have been our growth and prosperity. Well may the people of Allegheny County rejoice this day. And our rejoicing is not confined to our rapid strides in population and wealth. In education, refinement and good taste, we have kept pace with the march in commercial and manufacturing prosperity. For proof of this assertion I need only point to this edifice. Substantial as the basis of our wealth, elegant and faultless in its proportions, its symmetry and details, there it stands, the crowning achievement of the century! How beautifully appropriate that it should be finished in the centennial year, and be dedicated this day! Look at it, and rejoice, ye people of Allegheny County! Rejoice that in your abounding wealth you could be taxed two millions and a half for its erection, without feeling it, or even perceiving any increase of taxes. Rejoice that your public servants who made the contracts and expended the money were faithful and honest—not a dollar sticking to their fingers, and not a dollar going into the pockets of jobbers, pets or favorites. . . .

Standing on this eminence, like the temple in Jerusalem, it is the most conspicuous object in the city, and the first to arrest the eye

> *of a stranger. Like that temple, also, it is the pride of all the people; and hither, like God's chosen people, they will come at stated times, to hear the law and learn their duty as good citizens. Plain, chaste, unique in architecture, with no vain or superfluous ornaments, the eye never wearies tracing its lines of beauty and harmony. Founded on the living rock, solid and massive in structure, fire proof so far as granite, brick and iron can make a building fire proof, it will stand for ages to come.*

Charles E. Cornelius was introduced and read an original poem. Some of its 20 stanzas read as follows:

The Centennial Poem

Ye tow'ring hills whose faces stern
Look down upon our joyful rites,
In your scarred features may we learn
Of other days—forgotten sights.

. . . .

Once ye o'erlooked a verdant vale,
Thick clad in nature's garments green,
With tow'ring oak and beeches pale,
And sombre cypresses between.

. . . .

But lo! How quick the aspects change
When vandal men their presence show.
How their irreverent hands derange
All forms of nature here below!
The forest giants bite the dust,
The frightened birds and beasts retreat,
The grass is seared, the flowers crushed,
For quiet grove, comes noisy street.
Tall furnace stacks their flags of flame
Flaunt 'gainst a sky of leaden shade.
No tufts of velvet grass remain,
No willow copse, no cypress glade.

. . . .

And now, to crown the century's work,
A mile-stone set to mark the tread
Of Allegheny's sons along
The shining path by Progress led.
This noble pile uprears its front,
A sign to every age and land,
In the dear home of Liberty,
Progress and Law go hand in hand.

O Justice! Thou the attribute
Of Him from whom we count our days,
This temple grand, to thee we build,
And consecrate it to thy praise.
. . . .

By general request, and in response to the cries of ''Hayes'' from the audience on the platform and in the street, ex-President Rutherford B. Hayes ascended the rostrum and spoke. Judge Patton, who had presided over the first state court in the second Court House in 1841, then spoke. Rabbi L. Mayer offered a prayer. Rev. B. F. Woodburn closed the exercises with a benediction. So ended the official ceremonies.

The tower was now part of the city. The newspapers of the city spoke in praise of the great buildings. The national, popular voice of *Harper's Weekly* also reported the proceedings, but merely echoed the general local tone. There was no cynicism or disbelief; the national weekly told it nationally ''like it was'' locally:

In the celebration of the centennial of the organization of Allegheny County, Pennsylvania, there was nothing more gratifying than the local pride in the just completed court-house and jail. Naturally the jubilant demonstrations were stimulated by the wonderful prosperity of the county's great city of Pittsburgh; but there seems to have been amid all the noise and clatter of the occasion, a reverent feeling for the noblest and most beautiful public building in the country. The newspapers were full of the statistics of bituminous coal and iron, of Bessemer steel and glass, and of natural gas, but there was always a column for a restrained, understated pride in the fact that Pittsburgh had what its people are glad to believe was the supreme work of the greatest architect that the country has known. . . .

Pittsburgh and Albany are the only municipalities that gave the architect an opportunity for the manifestation of his genius, and the people of the former city regard their courthouse as Richardson's *monument.*

The Court House tower briefly dominated the city, but in this view, from c. 1900, the tall office buildings of the present-day city have already begun to appear. To the immediate left is the Carnegie Building (1895) by Longfellow, Alden & Harlow. Alexander Wadsworth Longfellow and Frank E. Alden had been in Richardson's office, and the Carnegie Building shows the Classical style that would soon drive Richardson Romanesque from fashion in Pittsburgh. To the far left is the Park Building (1896) by George B. Post. To the right of the Court House is the Post Office of 1891 by William Freret and James H. Windrim, which uses the popular tower-and-corner-pavilion arrangement also. Closer to the viewer, Victorian commercial buildings overlook the Monongahela Wharf.

THE TOWER ACHIEVED

THE COURT HOUSE AND JAIL IN 1888

With the aid of photographs it is not difficult to see how the County Buildings appeared to Pittsburghers. Large public buildings were the pride of cities throughout the western world. Elsewhere the law was similarly housed in similar pavilions. Jails had been constructed in connection with court houses the length and breadth of America. Towers abounded that signaled to the world the importance of city or county. But in the case of Pittsburgh the city and the world realized that a special grace and power inhered in Richardson's Court House and Jail; genius had molded the familiar contemporary forms into something superior and splendid.

Beyond the city, the most elevated opinion was that of Mariana Griswold Van Rensselaer (1851-1934). She was a well-known writer and critic of architecture, and also had been a personal friend of Richardson's. Her biography contains the closest in contemporary views that we possess. She writes:

Taken as a whole the design of this vast and complex structure, both inside and out, is a marvel of good sense as well as architectural beauty. None of the faults which appear in some of Richardson's other buildings can be found in this. It seems as simply yet completely right in execution as in first conception. We may take the Court-house as Richardson wished it to be taken—at the full expression of his mature power in the direction where it was most at home. . . . The Court-house is the most magnificent and imposing of his works, yet it is the most logical and quiet. It is the most somber and severe, yet it is the most original and in one sense the most eclectic. Although all its individual features have been drawn from an early southern style, its silhouette suggests some of the late-medieval buildings of the north of Europe, and its symmetry, its dignity, and nobility of air, speak of Renaissance ideals. To combine inspirations drawn from such different sources into a novel yet organic whole while expressing a complex plan of the most modern sort—this was indeed to be origi-

Overleaf left: the Court House when new.

Overleaf right: the County Buildings when new. In the right background, the towers of St. Paul's Cathedral; at the left, the tower of St. Peter's Episcopal Church. In 1901, St. Peter's was to be moved to another neighborhood and re-erected, so that the Frick Building could rise opposite the Court House. The slab-like skyscraper, completed in 1902, would end the Court House tower's dominance of the scene.

Right: the Ross Street entrance of the Court House, when new.

Below: the Grant Street entrances, showing their original proportions and the position of the lions.

Opposite: an early view of the grand stair in the Court House, with the entrance to the law library to the left.

Right: a brass lamp on the grand stair.

Below: the entrance to the grand stair, from the lobby at the original entrance level.

Left: the law library in the 1890s. The arch bears a side wall of the tower.

Below: a courtroom in the 1890s. The exposed iron-and-brick ceiling was standard in the courtrooms.

> *nal. There is no other municipal building like Richardson's Courthouse. It is as new as the needs it meets, as American as the community for which it was built. Yet it might stand without loss of prestige in any city of the world.*

Montgomery Schuyler, writing in 1911, also spoke in praise of the Allegheny County buildings:

> *One can only say that there is but one specimen of public architecture in downtown Pittsburgh which is much worth looking at or talking about and that, of course, is Richardson's group of the Court House and Jail. . . . Richardson did nothing, in civil architecture at least, more significant than this group. It fully bears out his description of it while it was still building, that of a "dignified pile of rocks." . . . This group is one of the chief ornaments of Pittsburgh. It would be among the chief ornaments of any American city fortunate enough to possess it.*

Schuyler died in 1914, and with him the last full voice in Richardson's praise. Although Richardson was still revered as one of the masters of American architecture it was not until the middle 1920s that a major critic could see Richardson in his full stature. This critic was Lewis Mumford. In a 1954 preface to a reissue of his *Sticks and Stones* (1924), Mumford confessed, "But even I, in 1924, had not yet appreciated the truly original qualities in Richardson's last work; so I repeated the old mistake of characterizing him as a mere romanticist."

At least in 1931, in *The Brown Decades,* Mumford had changed his opinion:

> *Henry Hobson Richardson, an architect who almost single-handed created out of a confusion which was actually worse than a mere void the beginnings of a new architecture. No single mind since Wren's has perhaps left such a large impression of his own personality, not alone through his work but through that of his disciples and successors; and no one has demonstrated better in practice the qualities that are necessary for a complete orchestration of all the personalities and forces concerned in building.*

By 1931, it was obvious that a full-fledged revival of interest in Richardson's work was well launched. If Mumford did not specifically mention the Pittsburgh buildings, an earlier admirer of Richardson, Henry-Russell Hitchcock, did speak of them with praise in 1927: "In his larger city buildings of intermediary order such as the Pittsburgh Court House and Jail he achieved a sense of large scale and impressive force that has hardly been equalled since his day." And later, in his Richardson monograph of 1936:

The Ross Street front of the Jail, from the north (left) and south (below).

The jail is more successful than the courthouse; but it was, of course, a much simpler thing for Richardson to design. The eight-foot voussoirs he had admired in Spain appear here, but the general impression is more like the granite buildings of the fifties in downtown Boston. The granite wall around the jail yard is one of the most magnificent displays of fine material in the world. The warden's house, with its lintelled windows set into one corner of this wall, is even more effective than that of Dance's famous old Newgate Prison in London. The towering end walls of the cross arms of the jail itself are equally impressive. The side walls are cut by tall arched windows like the sides of [a previously-mentioned non-Richardsonian design for an Alpine hospice], *but even bolder in scale.*

The octagonal central lantern and the square front tower, although splendidly scaled to the rest, reflect somewhat too specifically the fortified towns Richardson had seen the year before in Southern France. Some of the other little turrets are also an unnecessary complication, but they serve as ventilators. The bridge of sighs is at once barren and fussy beside the magnificent main entrance with its eight-foot voussoirs and pairs of narrow flanking lights. But these are minor faults.

Here, for once, Richardson had the opportunity to be as massive as he desired and, at the same time, perfectly expressive of the purpose of the building. The quality of the chimney shaft is rare in any age. But in the nineteenth century, which built so many smokestacks, this is perhaps the only one whose beauty is intentional and really architectural in the fullest sense. This plain cylindrical shaft rising above the solid wall, with its curious angles in plan, is of an abstract quality hardly dreamed of by twentieth century architects. Yet it is also absolutely material in its practical usefulness and its massive rock-faced granite. . . .

The court [of the Court House] *is all of great blocks of rock-faced granite and has no carved detail. Great arches flank two sides, scaled like a Roman aqueduct. Beneath these main arches other lintelled and arched lights are grouped. At the top of the projecting lower stories, which support terraces, are rows of smaller arches, three to each of the great arches below. Above the set-back are more arches and, above them, lintelled windows below the cornice. The end walls*

Above: a rear stair tower in the Court House courtyard. The upper part was intended as a ventilation exhaust.

Right: the Grant Street end of the courtyard, before it was converted to a park. The second level along the sides was the original first floor, with offices; the large semicircular windows above lighted mezzanines. The low arcades above lighted the corridors of the original second floor, devoted to courtrooms. Above this was a terrace, with courtroom clerestory windows behind.

have four stories of medium-sized arches and coupled lintelled windows at the top. The arches in the corner towers follow the line of the stairs.

This is a sort of engineering in masonry simpler even than the exterior of the Marshall Field [Wholesale Store] *begun the next year. It is as effectively open as the jail wall is effectively closed and impressive because of its enormous scale and its expressively varied rhythm. . . .*

There are significant changes from Richardson's earlier practice in the treatment of the exterior of the courthouse. There are indications of the increase of formality in design at this time. The symmetrical arrangement of this building is perhaps merely coincident with the acceptance of the Renaissance discipline by McKim, Mead, and White at just this time. The use of light-coloured granite throughout. . . makes plain that he was tiring of exterior polychromy and consciously initiating the monochrome manner of treatment McKim, Mead, and White were so soon to impose on American architecture generally. In the jail, with its magnificent rough granite surfaces, this was desirable. But the exterior of the courthouse, perhaps, has a certain impoverished look. . . .

This effect is of small importance. As Richardson was aware, the Pittsburgh atmosphere soon turned the walls to an even tone of blackish grey. More serious is the character of the masonry, with very narrow courses alternating with rather wide courses. . . . This gives a monotonous horizontal pattern to the walls fortunately not imitated in the jail or the great tower. It may have some constructive significance in bonding the walls together more solidly. But it certainly seems to reflect the rise of a more mechanical feeling for design, associated with the substitution of wash renderings for the free pen work of Stanford White and Langford Warren. This newer sort of rendering was probably introduced to the office by John Shepley and Charles A. Coolidge, who came to take Langford Warren's place at this time. In it the walls were very pale and the windows washed with black ink. Thus they looked like holes in the wall, exactly the thing Richardson had previously tried to avoid by the use of small-paned windows.

The detail on the exterior of this building is very restrained, but also very archaeological. The rich rough material is quite without smooth-cut detail like that on the jail or in the court. Nor is there a profusion of free ornament as on Austin Hall [Harvard, 1881-83], *but rather an effect of stiffness and coldness completely lacking in Richardson's previous work. On top of the tower, at the furthest point from the eye, the detail grows more elaborate. But it is the tall shaft of the tower between the cornice of the main building and the belfry story with its rounded projections at the corners and in the middle of each side, which is the best thing on the exterior.*

> *The side elevations, however, have great distinction when seen as a whole. The lintelled openings in the lower stories are of the type introduced on the side facade of the Albany City Hall* [of 1880-82]. *They are here used in a much more consistent way. The great arches of the main floor really give a remarkably open effect. The lintelled windows below the cornice and in the gable are of the . . . type* [that Richardson had used in several library stacks]. *The low vaulted entrance lobby has a Piranesian grandeur very superior to the intricate interweaving of the half flights in the Western Staircase of the Albany Capitol, as it was planned at this time.*

After 1936, there was no extended notice of the Pittsburgh buildings until I published an article, "The Romanesque Revival in Pittsburgh," in 1957. Interest in the work of Richardson had become widespread so that a further consideration of the Court House and Jail was timely. We may quote it as indicative of the interest in the structures at that time.

> *Although the style of the building is generally Southern French Romanesque, it is very evident here that the personal manner of Richardson, even at its most archaeological, shows borrowings from*

A modern view of the Grant Street entrances.

many other sources. . . . The general form of the Court House, obviously a re-working of the Albany State House scheme, is early French Renaissance. In this instance one may note the application of one revived style to another building type: it is as if a Romanesque skin had been pulled over the Renaissance body. However, even that skin is not purely Romanesque and it is spotted and colored with elements from other periods, notably the three cavernous Syrian arches of the main entrance and the dormers which are late French Gothic in form. The detailing is archaeologically correct, but even here there is a Byzantine quality subtly combined with the Romanesque, which is apparent in the sculptured capitals of the windows and entrance archways. The Bridge of Sighs which connects the Court House and Jail was doubtless inspired in function by its Venetian namesake, although in form it favors the Rialto.

The great triple windows of the corner pavilions owe nothing to historical precedent; they are purely late 19th-century features, large areas of glass designed to give as much light as possible to modern court rooms. The building is eclectic in a very wide sense and not limited to the narrow confines of one revived style.

Three courtroom windows on the original second floor, with windows of the original third floor above. This is a detail of one of the corner pavilions.

The great tower whose clean, boldly-molded flanks rise straight from the entrance facade is an example of the persistence of the Spanish Romanesque element in Richardson's personal style. It is, in essence, a tremendous elongation of the Trinity tower and is the last of his works to show the influence of the Spanish lantern churches. The four angle turrets with the ornamental bull's eyes reminiscent of the Collegiata of Toro are particularly Spanish. However, the elaborate belfry arcades, which recall those of the Albany City Hall, are French.

The inner courtyard is almost free from Romanesque historicisms and its fenestration rivals that of the [Marshall Field Wholesale Store].

The best feature of the interior is the main staircase which rises from the basement to the third [present fifth] *floor in short broad flights, not too elaborately interwoven, and supported and adorned by massive arches of cut Bedford limestone. Again, except for some carved capitals on the low pillars supporting the arches, the ornament is restrained and the simple voussoirs give a quality of clean simplicity to the design.*

Below: a balustrade on the grand stair.

Opposite: a view up the grand stair. The masonry is of limestone; Richardson had originally been considering brownstone for the purpose.

Opposite: the grand stair seen from the present fourth-floor level. The space is terminated by a plain ceiling of brick segmental arches on rolled iron beams.

Left: an impost on the grand stair.

Below: a view downward to the original entrance lobby and upward to the law library.

> *Of the two Pittsburgh buildings, the Jail now seems to be in the greater aesthetic favor possibly because, aside from its generally Romantic outline and mass, it has almost no stylistic detailing and because it expresses so eminently its function. It is very abundantly and superlatively a jail. It is also probably the most masculine, rugged and solid of Richardson's designs. The massive walls of the jail yard with their great blocks of Milford granite recall Mycenaean masonry and they appeal strongly to that nostalgia for the gigantic and the primitive which is so much a part of the modern sensibility. . . .*
>
> *The details of the building do not suffer by comparison with the ensemble. The ranges of granite along the principal facade are broken by few openings; chief among them are the main entrance, a low arch with huge eight-foot voussoirs (reminiscent of portals that Richardson had seen on his Spanish journey in 1882), and the windows of the warden's house. As Hitchcock suggests, the overall silhouette of the building recalls the fortified towns which Richardson had seen in southern France, especially the square tower near the main door which reminds one of those of the Valentre Bridge at Cahors. The octagonal dome over the crossing of the cell block wings seems to have been inspired not so much by the cupolas of southern France as by those of the Lombard or Rhenish Romanesque. One feature of the composition that is unmistakably 19th century is the tall chimney in the jail yard, a splendidly proportioned column of granite with a suggestion of medieval corbelling at the top.*
>
> *The plan of the interior of the Jail proper with its four wings (originally three) radiating from the central space under the octagonal dome has obviously been inspired by the plan of the Syrian church of St. Simeon Stylites (A.D. 450-70) which was illustrated in de Vogüé's book,* La Syrie Centrale, *a copy of which was in Richardson's library. One is also reminded of the Octagon of Ely Cathedral and the plan of James Wyatt's Fonthill Abbey, but it is very doubtful if these buildings influenced Richardson in any way. The interiors of the wings themselves are high gaunt halls which rise some sixty feet from floor to roof and which are lighted in dramatic fashion by tall round-arched windows. Five tiers of cell blocks occupy the center of each wing. The four wings converge like cathedral naves on the great echoing void under the dome.*

In 1958, Hitchcock wrote, in *Architecture Nineteenth and Twentieth Centuries,* that

> *the Allegheny County Buildings. . . consist of a vast quadrangular courthouse dominated by a very tall tower that rises in the center of the front and a gaol across the street to the rear. Except for the courtyard walls, interesting for the variety and the openness of their ranges of granite arcading, the courthouse offers on the whole only a sort*

Left: the interior of the Jail rotunda today.

Below: the plan of the Jail, published in 1888. The chimney was moved close to the obtuse angle in the outer wall to the right in actual construction.

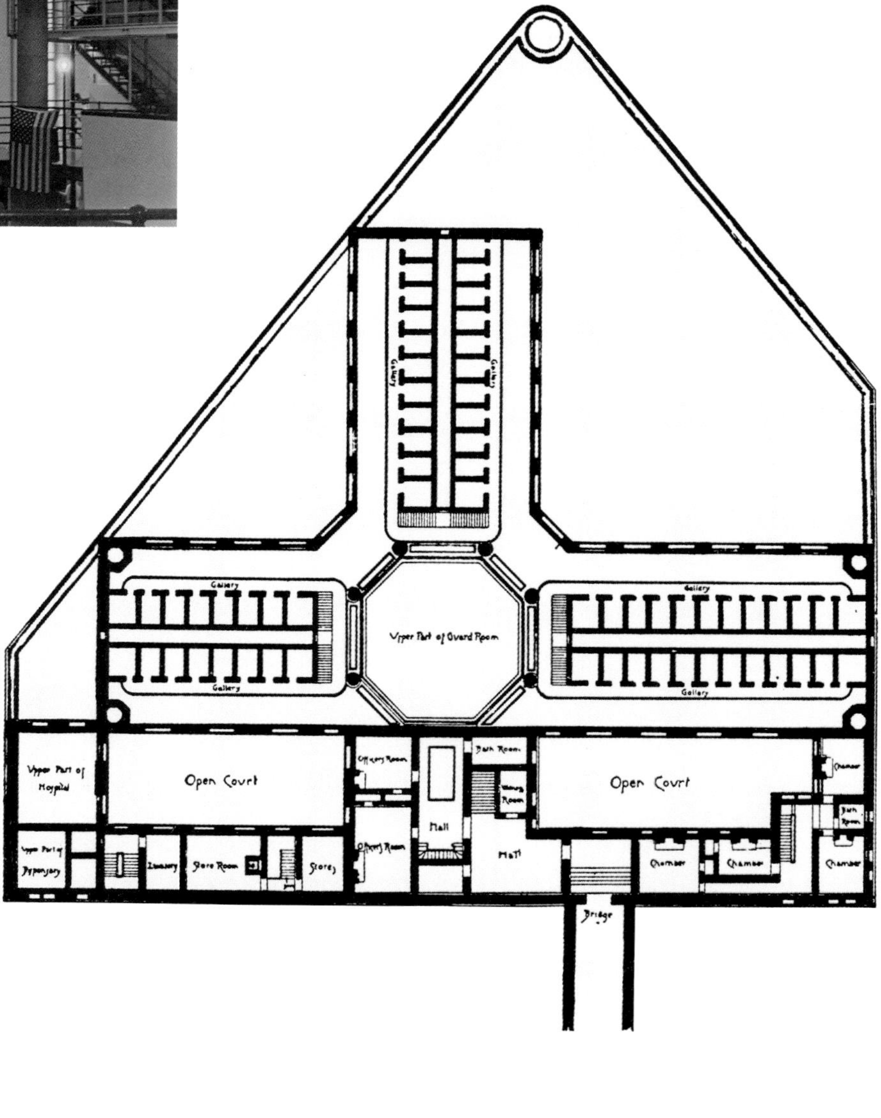

> *of summary of his talents; the detail, above all, is afflicted with an archaeological dryness that must be due to the increasing dependence of his assistants on published documents of medieval carving. The courthouse provided, however, the model for many large public buildings in the next few years. Among these, the City Hall in Minneapolis, Minn., begun by the local firm of Long & Kees in 1887, is not unworthy of comparison with the original, particularly as regards the tower. That of Toronto in Canada, built by E. J. Lennox in 1890-91, is less interesting but even more monumental; it also signified the supersession of English by American influence in Canadian architecture at this point, as does the almost equally Richardsonian Windsor Station begun by the American Bruce Price in 1888.*
>
> *The Pittsburgh Jail is a masterpiece of the most personal order, Piranesian in scale, nobly expressive of its gloomy purpose and as superb an example of granite masonry as exists in the world. It epitomizes Richardson's genius where the courthouse merely summarizes his talents.*

By altering the position of the tower from the courtyard to the Grant Street side of the Court House, Richardson causes it to rise sheer from the front steps and to house the central portal at its base. This revision gave it much more effectiveness in the overall design, though it darkened the interior of the Law Library. The essay by Edwin Hetherington describes other aspects of the Court House and Jail:

> *The red tiles of the steep* [Court House] *roof now turned a grimy black, at one time complemented the pinkish-gray granite of the exterior walls. The individual parts of the building, like the dormers, pavilions, or side bays, have their own roofs, but all penetrate one another, thus tending to unify the various large elements within a restrained outline. The towers with their granite roofs rise above this outline in a picturesque fashion. The pyramidal shape of their roofs serves as a leitmotif to link them formally to each other and to the large tiled roofs of the corner pavilions below.*
>
> *The consistent use of Milford granite, mostly rock-faced with cut trim and decoration, also unifies the surface of the exterior. Richardson's elimination of polychromy, Hitchcock believed, gives the courthouse "a certain impoverished look." Of course Pittsburgh's atmosphere precluded a more colorful treatment of the walls. Furthermore, occasional passages of polychromy would probably have seemed out of place in a building of such massive dignity and huge scale. Instead, Richardson enlivened the surface through varied stonework alone. The building, for the most part, is composed of alternating wide and narrow bands of masonry which transform the walls into "a monotonous horizontal pattern," according to Hitchcock,* [though he] *concedes that the stones are arranged in this fashion to assure*

the solidity of the walls, because the narrow courses are bonded with the brick backing, unlike the wider and shallower bands. To describe the stonework as "monotonous," however, does not give it full justice. Since the roofs do not compose an even cornice line, the string courses, water-tables, and horizontal bands of masonry organize the surface as they. . . follow [the] *various projections and recessions* [of the building]. *Random ashlar* [for instance], *combined with a discontinuous cornice and the inter-penetrating masses of the whole, would have articulated the exterior in a confused manner. Also, the horizontality fully complements the restful symmetry of each aspect of the composition. As a practical matter, since the individual blocks of granite were shaped at Milford and numbered to indicate their exact position in the wall before going to Pittsburgh, it would have been very expensive and difficult to build in random ashlar. Finally, the regularity of the stonework allowed Richardson to enhance the decorative and expressive value of the openings, one of his primary considerations. The large voussoirs of the triple entrance, for example, stand out dramatically against the horizontal bands, thereby increasing the dignity and, seemingly, the size of these arches. The voussoirs also create distinct decorative patterns over groups of openings where the stones impinge upon one another, and therefore, in a single example, bind the individual window closely to the others in the same group.*

Since the color of the stone and the amount of cut trim are both restrained, the texture of the granite becomes very important. The roughness of each block suggests the unusual strength of the walls. Light falling over the rock-face granite enlivens the surface, and creates a sober contrast between the carved and finished stonework and the natural texture of the surrounding walls. The carving is, of course, relatively sparse in keeping with [Richardson's] *desire to avoid sooty disfigurement. Also, the preponderance of rock-face granite and the proportionately small amount of detail are exactly consistent with his pursuit of an architectural effect dependent upon the overall outline of the building, rather than upon sudden passages of disruptive detail. The varied stonework around the openings stresses their identity but does not interfere with the unified conception of the whole building.*

In short, the primary decorative interest lies in the pattern of the windows and the texture of the stone. What carving there is, however restrained in amount, is actually quite varied. Studies for capitals of columns near the windows show that each one is different from the rest in detail. Yet, all have approximately the same size and flatness. Thus, even the most diverse particulars of the exterior are given an identifiable unity. Richardson learned the restraint of detail from his recent trip to Europe, where he saw that elaborate medieval carving was usually restricted to certain areas in a building, such as capitals and decorative courses. The one shortcoming of the carved details at Pittsburgh is that they become most elaborate in the higher parts of the building where they are farthest from the eye, as Hitchcock notes. In the main tower, for example, the faces cut on the row of dentils immediately under the belfry or the foliate decoration of the capitals and cornices are almost imperceptible, even when viewed from the upper parts of the courthouse.

The side elevations were executed according to the designs of the competition, with only some changes in fenestration. The seven windows of the third story of each pavilion and the central gable were reduced to five. Single-arched lights flank the carriageways, instead of two, and square-headed windows open the third story between the corner pavilions and the projecting round bays. The windows on top of these last elements have been replaced by bands of ornamental stonework, which are inconspicuously located well above street level. These bays introduce a note of plasticity into an otherwise long, flat wall between the two end pavilions, while capturing light for and conveying the presence of the offices contained within them. Their slightly elevated eaves suggest the continuity of the pavilions' cornice line all the way along the side elevation. These bays, together with the central gables, accentuate the presence of the carriageways and, consequently, of a transverse axis of the courthouse. . . .

The Ross Street side of the building also matches the competition designs quite closely. The balustrades between the small dormers of the central section have been removed, and the number of windows across the third story has been reduced. The only other change was that the arch of the entrance was lowered so that it no longer impinges upon the first-story string course. As a result the windows for the female witness room above the Ross Street entrance receive hardly any light from the outside.

The courtyard, too, was executed as the original designs prescribed, except completely in rock-face granite instead of brick with some granite trim. The only other change was the elimination of a balcony at one end on the second story. At the Grant Street end, individual rows of arched and lintelled windows look into the grand stairway. Around the other three sides, the windows of the basement and first story are grouped under the repeated arch of the carriageway, as . . . in the competition designs. The large scale of the arcade, superimposed with rows of smaller arched openings, and the deliberate suppression of almost all carved detail are distinctly reminiscent of great Roman aqueducts. Just as they were beautifully functional spans to carry water, Richardson's courtyard walls, with the most purposive directness, admit plenty of light to the interior. The windows of the corner towers clearly express the ascending turns of the stairs. Since the courtyard is virtually free from any but the most general stylistic historicisms, the rhythm of the numerous windows, the contrast of arched voussoirs set against rectilinear courses of stone, and the texture of the rock-face granite itself all assume a decorative role, which sums up Richardson's primary consideration in regard to architectural effect.

In plan, all the floors closely followed the competition designs. Changes of the first story included. . . the rearrangement of the piers of the lower part of the grand stairway. On the second floor, the new location of the main tower changed the shape of the law library, whose walls became thick to support the tower's weight. Also, the glazed wall looking into the stairway had to be eliminated, and on the third floor the Supreme Court-room was moved into one of the pavilions. [By 1907, when a new set of plans was made,] *many of the rooms of this level had already been re-adapted to the new needs of the county. The roof story was closed when Richardson ended the corner stairs on the third floor, and on all levels encaustic tile replaced ornate flooring shown in the competition design.*

The best feature of the interior is the grand stairway, composed of wide, low arches of cut Bedford limestone and broad flights of stairs. The three entrances (now filled in and decorated with flags as a war memorial) and the vaulted vestibule open at the foot of the stairway. From its second landing, two short flights diverge and climb to the first-story mezzanine. Two other flights continue up to the front of the law library where they join into a single flight turning to the second story, whose mezzanine creates a huge void at the summit of the stairway. At either side on each level are the corner stairs and the brightly lit corridors, whose walls are wainscoted in polished marble. In general, the arrangement of the interior, with the grand stairway rising vertically and opening to long horizontal hallways, is comparable to the exterior whose tower stands above the low mass spreading beneath it.

Richardson probably had little to do with the interior carving since he died half way through construction. Details were usually designed when the building was nearly complete, as the blank capitals of the working plans would seem to indicate. These were later decorated by the stonecarving firm of Evans and Tombs of Boston, who executed the details of many of the architect's buildings. Whether or not Richardson saw the details, they are very much in his idiom, and restricted to just a few areas around and within the grand stairway. The limestone piers have capitals of flat, intricate motifs of leaves and flowers. The freestanding columns have wide foliate capitals of granite consistent with the broad dimensions of the polished shafts. Even the limestone balusters of the marble-topped railings have tiny capitals of amazing variety. Since the contract for the furnishing of offices and courtrooms was let under Shepley, Rutan and Coolidge, the interiors of these rooms, now much altered, are of little interest in regard to Richardson.

Before making the final design of the prison footbridge, the architect did numerous drawings to study the rhythm of ascending and descending windows and the various effects of different wall surfaces and roof lines, all above the continuous sweep of a low arch. The bridge, as executed, offers a compromise between these studies. A low gable distinguishes its summit while the flat roof is hidden behind the wall. The rectilinear silhouette of the upper part contrasts in shape with the arch below. The small lintelled windows rise toward the central arched window with its multiple reveals, which again emphasize the middle and highest portion of the bridge. The walls are constructed of alternate bands of rock-face masonry, in the manner of the courthouse, against which the voussoirs of the central window and those of the bridge's arch serve as ornamental features, along with the small bands of dentils and the cut copings of the wall.

Richardson probably planned a footbridge between the two buildings from the very earliest designs. A study for the jail shows a bridge in approximately the same position as it was executed. Also, an entrance was to be on axis with the courthouse while an octagonal guard room was shifted to the south. Two wings entered the central room at forty-five degree angles, and the third entered directly from the rear corner of the site. Along Ross Street were aligned the service and administrative rooms and the jailer's house. Behind this last part, situated at the northern end of the site, was a separate building, possibly a chapel. From this early study, Richardson developed the competition design, which had both the entrance and guard room on the main axis of the courthouse and each of the wings intersecting the central void at ninety degrees. From this design to the construction of the jail, only minor changes occurred. Some of the rooms along Ross Street were rearranged. The eastern wing of cells was cut off squarely where it intersected the surrounding wall, and the floor of the guard room inside the octagon was removed to create an open space from the basement to the roof. Finally the chimney of the boiler room was moved next to the service driveway.

Where the cell blocks radiate from the guard room, tall granite columns with octagonal cushion capitals ascend from the first floor to the height of the fifth tier of cells. Above the arches, whose lines are reinforced by simple moldings, the walls rise into an irregular octagonal dome lighted by four windows. The cell blocks stand within iron galleries and completely free of the exterior walls. Light floods in through the tall windows, over forty feet in height, from the exercise yards of the jail.

In general, Richardson's prison is successful from a functional viewpoint, and this is quite remarkable considering he had little or no experience in the design of jails. Van Rensselaer reports [as we have seen] *that the architect's first concerns were "convenience, security, and thorough ventilation." Of these three, Richardson fell short of his usual standard of excellence on the last feature. Hot air collects in the upper portions of the vast interior while the lower cells are relatively cool. The jail is essentially a detention prison, in contrast to a large workhouse for convicted criminals, and as such, must accommodate a wide variety of inmates, including some falsely accused of crime who are awaiting trial to prove their innocence. Individual cells, Richardson believed, were the best means to segregate these various types. Larger units, such as dormitories, are for stable groups of similarly classified prisoners, and therefore, would have been impractical because of the high turnover of different inmates at the Allegheny County Jail. The prisoners can be most easily classified in single cells arranged as interior blocks and opening into a central guard room to make observation relatively easy. Security becomes a more important factor when the units are placed along the exterior walls. The inside cells make escape highly difficult as do the surrounding walls of the jail and the restricted entry. Richardson probably intended to have the inmates fed in their cells, thus emphasizing the strict segregation of types. The greatest difficulty in supervision occurs during exercise periods, when the prisoners mingle in the yards and guard room. This problem arose because of the insufficient size of the jail site and not because of Richardson's design. He endeavored, at least, to separate males and females; but even so, many prisoners must be personally supervised when they are out of their cells. On the whole, however, the jail proved Richardson's ability to overcome problems in utilitarian design, and even today its outstanding qualities are security and relative ease of administration.*

On the exterior, Richardson had suppressed alternate bands of masonry in favor of regular wide courses that gradually become narrower toward the top. The result of a flat wall broken only by occasional lintelled windows and arched doorways is an unusually strong and powerful effect. There is no detail except the machicolation of the entrance, bridge tower, central octagon, and chimney, and the huge eight foot voussoirs of the entrances. These stones emphasize the only two passages into the jail and present a sober pattern against an otherwise very horizontal wall. The large, rectangular blocks of granite, like the voussoirs, are rock-face and form a magnificent expression of severe, enclosed space. The rugged grandeur of this wall architecture is unequalled in any other work by Richardson.

Above these massive lower parts, the jail presents its rather picturesque outline. The central octagon dominates the whole, and the small turrets, where fresh air is drawn into the jail, accentuate the gabled extremities of the northern and southern wings. Like the courthouse, the red tile of the roofs must at one time have complement-

ed the tone of the Milford granite which covers the cell wings in regular courses. The pattern of tall, arched windows modifies the horizontality of the wings, and the chimney of the boiler room adds a pronounced vertical note to the entire composition. Furthermore, its curved surface contrasts with the rectilinearity of the other parts of the jail, while its material and machicolation link it stylistically with the rest.

The massive, enclosed character of the jail is unlike the more open and imponderous quality of the courthouse. The latter structure expresses its plan in its fenestration, but the plain wall of the jail gives little hint of its interior. The windows of the sheriff's house or those of the cell blocks that peer over the wall convey the presence of these interior features, but on the whole, the jail's rough-hewn walls in themselves are the most important and interesting aspect of the exterior. Also, its picturesque outline and asymmetry contrast with the formal regularity of the courthouse. In the larger building and in the placement of the smaller one, Richardson seems to have drawn on his Beaux-Arts background which dictated grand, axial schemes in design. The jail by itself reflects the Victorian, Romantic aspect of Richardson's artistic temperament, in its picturesqueness and its expression as a ''massive symbol of incarceration.'' The rock-face blocks of masonry and oversized voussoirs, the large, flat architectural elements, and the severity of treatment are all generally comparable to the Carceri *series of etchings by Piranesi, a highly romantic artist of the eighteenth century, whose pictures Richardson may have appreciated when he designed Allegheny County Jail. In short, the jail, in its massiveness, confinement, and geometric simplicity, contrasts with the more open and ornamental exterior of the courthouse. Yet the axial planning and the similarity of materials bind the two buildings together, so that they balance one another artistically and thereby create one of the most uniquely interesting architectural projects of the nineteenth century.*

As well as differing formally, the two structures are founded on distinct spatial conceptions. In a word, the jail is closed; the courthouse open. This quality of the latter is best demonstrated by the grand stairway. Although its layout is fairly easy to describe, the experience of its space is more complex. As one mounts the stairs, the piers and columns seem to move and interpenetrate, and the vista into the courtyard through the large windows constantly changes. At the landings, one has the choice of numerous directions of horizontal movement. Thus, the stairway defines space in two ways: by broad flights of steps, it denotes various degrees of restrained ascent or descent, and through transparent walls and interpenetrating masses, it suggests imaginary movement. The experience of these two is, of course, dependent on motion by which forms are viewed in succession. The forthright bulk of masonry construction hampers complete spatial fluidity, but Richardson, by moving the main tower forward, opened up the stairway a great deal. In doing so, he imbued the stairway with a sense of "space-permeability," derived from the relative freedom of movement up the stairs and from the light and air entering from the courtyard. At a simpler level, Richardson proved his concern for space within the courthouse by the logical and functional layout of rooms and by his insistence upon proper ventilation and illumination throughout the interior. To have eliminated the stairway the architect would have shown his ability to envelop a controlled, comprehensible space. By including this important feature, Richardson added an indefinite fluidity of space that tends to break down internal divisions and the visual distinction between interior and exterior.

Across Ross Street, there is the same rational planning but the space is changed. The guard room and wings create a huge church-like interior. Yet the sense of void is limited to the central portion because the wings are filled by the cell blocks. Also, displacing most of the floor area, the cells and their narrow galleries restrict movement and consequently the experience of space. Furthermore, both the location of cell blocks very near the windows, however large they might be, and the network of bars covering all openings tend to deny any suggestion of spatial fluidity. Finally, the severe treatment of the surrounding jail walls clearly defines inside and outside. In short, the jail literally becomes a "space-trap."

Both county buildings are massive, horizontal structures with a predominance of flat surfaces that restrain plasticity. These characteristics signify Richardson's simple, yet broad treatment of the project. The scale of the buildings, like Richardson's own stature, is huge, as the few dimensions mentioned in the competition designs indicate, and this and both the weight and balance of the masses produce an overwhelming sense of monumentality. There are neither eruptions of energy nor struggles between parts. All are solidly ordered and quietly related to one another. Within this structural context, Richardson created the effects of spatial differentiation. In the jail, the qualities of stability and closed space complement one another. In the courthouse, on the other hand, where Richardson tried to open masonry construction as much as possible, solid massiveness and space-permeability would seem to be partial antitheses. That Richardson has fully synthesized the two demonstrates his power of design and the vigorous expression of his buildings.

The Commissioners were motivated in the selection of an architect by a desire to display the high esteem in which they held Allegheny County. The grandeur of Richardson's courthouse and jail did not disappoint their expectations, for it conveys the civic importance of Pittsburgh and surrounding communities. In particular, the court-

house and tower, in their height and symmetry, signify the authority of local judicial power, and the jail embodies the awesome severity of incarceration. These ''poetic''connotations are the culmination of Richardson's purpose of architectural expression, throughout the buildings. He began with the plan of the courthouse which consists essentially of large, important rooms alternating with smaller, subsidiary chambers around an open rectangle. His concern for light and air dictated that he place the major rooms in the corners and along the free sides of the rectangle. From this simple layout he molded the elevation in flat surfaces, whose horizontal differentiation, along Diamond Street and Fifth Avenue, indicates five important interior elements, and along Grant and Ross Streets, three internal elements. As the next step, he determined the size and shape of windows according to the interior need and the hierarchial importance of rooms. The distinction of windows complemented the planar differentiation of the elevation. Finally, Richardson embellished the exterior with some stylistic historicisms, but rarely do they hamper the basic expression of interior plan. In the jail, the same process occurred. Security, convenience and ventilation determined the plan and both the general and the particular aspects of the elevation. As a result of this consistency of design, the jail signifies its purpose and use.

This practice was unlike that of many of Richardson's predecessors and contemporaries, who decided what a building should look like from the outside and subsequently arranged the interior as best as possible according to the preestablished position of walls and windows. Richardson transformed these last elements into units expressive of inside layout. For example, the rectangular walls and arched windows of the corner stair towers reflect both the interior flights of stairs rising at right angles and the square shape of the elevator shaft. The granite of the walls and roof gives this utilitarian expression a medieval character but in no way detracts from the lucidity of the design.

In the same fashion that he made the exterior correspond to the interior, Richardson designed his buildings in relation to their respective sites. The rectangular lot of the courthouse permitted a symmetrical arrangement of parts, whereas the irregular shape of the site behind almost required an asymmetrical deposition of architectural elements.

Similarly, he has successfully adapted his boldly utilitarian plans to his chosen historical style—the Romanesque. The stair towers, just described and the main tower, employed as storage space and ventilating snorkels, exemplify this aspect of the project. Their silhouettes have a picturesque quality that enhances their useful character. In a description written to accompany a project at the very end of his life, Richardson expressed his belief that the Romanesque was "especially adapted to the requirements of civic buildings; for while it maintains its dignity together with a strong sense of solidity, it lends itself at the same time most readily to the requirements of utility." Thus in the county buildings, Richardson has attempted to break down the usual dichotomy between what is purely practical and functional and what is aesthetically pleasing. Some romantic spirit has been infused into the highly utilitarian.

Of course, the heaviness of masonry construction itself helps to create a sense of solidity and dignity. In construction, Richardson insisted upon a high standard of craftsmanship and the buildings do, indeed, convey the structural integrity of the chosen materials, mainly stone, brick and iron. Compatible with the broad treatment of structure is the restrained ornament. The larger units of decoration, such as the pattern of stones and the rhythm of openings, do not disrupt the stability of interpenetrating masses. Nor do the specific passages of smaller details, like carved capitals and bands, detract from the effective quietness of the overall silhouette or from the monumental strength of larger forms.

In short, because of "his power in general conception," every feature of the courthouse and jail has been given some distinction of its own, but each is subservient to an overall architectural effect. Through gradation of parts and their integration into a whole, Richardson has demonstrated how all aspects of the project relate appropriately to one another. For example, the courthouse relates to the jail and each to its respective site; the exterior of each to its interior layout; or the scale of the buildings to their civic importance. Furthermore, decoration is consistent with structure; mass, with space; and utility, with historical style. All these things are coherently adapted to formulate a sense of organic unity.

We have presented here the documents in the case of the Court House and Jail. Much has been written—most of it in praise—and much more will probably be written on the form of the buildings as they appeared in 1888. It would appear now that these structures are still splendid—the tower even more than ever triumphant. But now, to keep the record straight, we must consider the subsequent history of the buildings to the present day.

THE TOWER AND THE CITY

1889-1913

Once the tower had been completed, it existed quietly for a season on the glory conferred upon it by the city. It glowed, it shone; for a time it seemed quite sufficient for the County's needs. The records of the early 1890s contain only small references to finishing touches or minor alterations.

An alteration in the original layout of the County Buildings is recorded in the *Minutes* of April 16, 1892:

The power house is being moved from its location in the Jail yard next to Diamond Street in order to make more economical use of the Jail area, to secure greater quiet and comfort in certain parts of the Jail, and to insure more space within the walls for an addition when needed. The power house will be moved to the lot owned by the County opposite Diamond Street. This requires the construction of a new building, since the one presently on the lot is inadequate.

There seems to be some doubt about the implementation of this plan, because the power installations appear to have still been in their original place in 1904 when the Jail additions were finally begun. The *Minutes* of July 5, 1894 state that the Commissioners awarded a local architect, Charles Bickel, $2,450 for a set of plans. This entry is also of interest because it shows that additions to the Jail were already contemplated as early as 1892.

Early in November 1894, the Thirty-third Annual Convention of the American Institute of Architects was held in Pittsburgh, and the County Buildings together with the steel mills were the chief points of interest for the visiting designers. The Pittsburgh *Bulletin,* reporting on the convention, wrote that, "in our noble Court House there is embodied a worthy and enduring memorial in imperishable granite to H. H. Richardson. . . . It is such a work that makes even ordinary mortals wish that they were great architects."

Opposite: the Court House tower rises about 325 feet above Grant Street: the last and arguably the greatest of the distinguished series of towers by Richardson.

This complimentary statement was echoed in the general approbation manifested toward the Court House and Jail by the world at large. The esteem in which the County Buildings were held by those admirers outside the city is evident through the manner in which they came to the defence of the Court House when it was threatened with mutilation in 1904.

Meanwhile, the area around the County Buildings was subjected to one major change—the erection of the 21-story Frick Building in 1901-02, which was at the time the largest steel-frame building in the city. With its metal cage enclosed in a severe Neo-Classical envelope, it marks the emergence of the great slab skyscraper in Pittsburgh. The Frick Building is massive and powerful in both form and detail; in spirit it is related to the County Buildings. The Frick Building is also well suited to the age of the Pittsburgh industrialist; in fact, the building leaves little doubt that Henry Clay Frick (1849-1919), one of Pittsburgh's industrial leaders, intended it as a monument to his financial might.

This great impenetrable slab changed the aspect of the Court House. No longer did the soaring tower, the symbol of the majesty of the law, front grandly toward the west. Although the distance in feet between the capstone of the tower and the over-riding cornice of the skyscraper is minimal, the gulf between the values symbolized by one and the technological force represented by the other is immeasurable. Here the modern dilemma is made manifest in a dramatic confrontation that even Richardson could not have envisioned. Physically, the Court House did not stand a chance. The Frick Building initiated those constant changes in scale of the "downtown" city. The colossal is piled upon the gigantic. For the moment, this ascension rests with the 68-story Cor-Ten bulk of the USX Tower. But amid this procession from scale to scale, the upraised minatory finger of the Court House holds its own; the spirit of it is not only beyond tragedy, but beyond technology.

The County Buildings began to be plagued by the constant American phenomenon: lack of space to accommodate the services needed by an expanding population. What had seemed to Thomas Mellon and his fellow protestors highly unjustified, and to the dedicated County Commissioners of the 1880s highly sufficient, had become by 1900 supremely lacking. The Court House and Jail were too small for the County's needs. As early as 1899, *The Engineering News* had reported that "the commissioners of Allegheny County are considering the advisability of building a fourth story on the Court House." Not less pressing was the matter of additions to the Jail. The *Commercial Gazette* recorded on January 4, 1900 that "the Prison Board will meet on Saturday in regular session to consider improvements to the Jail, an increase in the number of employees, and a general line of reconstruction." The *Gazette* reported again on January 27 that

there was an Allegheny County Prison Board meeting yesterday. It

Opposite: Richardson stonewalled: the Frick Building has confronted the Court House tower since 1902. Its architects were the prominent D. H. Burnham & Company of Chicago.

> *was a special meeting to consider proposals to alter the Jail. The board decided to spend about $22,000 for alterations. No other definite action was taken except to appoint F. J. Osterling as the architect to prepare plans of the alterations and to submit them later.*

Submit them he did. Frederick J. Osterling was a local Richardsonian disciple, but had not been taught by the Master himself. It was Osterling, in fact, who gave the Jail its final form but he did it so sympathetically that his additions are practically indistinguishable from the old. His pious regard for the established fabric of the Jail was and is exemplary.

In 1901 Osterling received a commission to design the Allegheny County Mortuary. Although the Mortuary is an undistinguished pedestrian structure, Richardsonian more in manner than in spirit, it has adequately performed its dolorous function for many years. In 1928, the Mortuary was moved to its present position on Fourth Avenue to make way for the present County Office Building.

After 1900, the question of additions to the Court House and Jail became more pressing. Two proposals were considered: constructing an annex on the plot bounded by Diamond Street, Fourth Avenue, and Grant and Ross Streets; or adding two or more floors to the existing Court House. Both views were presented in an article in the *Gazette* on August 22, 1902.

> *At an informal discussion, Judge Frazer is reported to have expressed the opinion that a couple of stories should have been added to the present building some time ago. When architects were consulted about this, they said it could not have been done without injury to the architectural beauty of the building.*
>
> *When the present Court House was built twelve years ago, it was thought to be capable of caring for the increased business of the County for the next half century. Now the officials are all complaining of being over-crowded. They say that by putting the courts, and offices of the Clerks of Courts, prothonotary and register in the new building, the space would be sufficient for many years to come.*

The Commissioners did not however adopt the plan providing for the new building. Despite public disclaimer, County officials seemed to favor altering the existing building. The Board of County Commissioners were not so much impressed by aesthetic considerations as they were by expediency—a notable contrast to the ideals of the Board which helped to create the Court House.

The question of the expansion of the Jail was much simpler; it was merely a matter of extending the existing building to occupy the block bounded by Diamond, Sixth, and Fifth Avenues, and Ross Street. The *Gazette* of December 1, 1908 reported:

> *With the new wing and additions the Jail will be one of the most*

Richardson travestied: the Allegheny County Mortuary of 1901 imitates the dormers and the Ross Street entrance of the Court House and the bridge tower of the Jail in a bulky composition by the local architect Frederick John Osterling. Originally the Mortuary stood opposite the Jail on Diamond Street, but in 1928 it was moved bodily one block south.

complete in the country and will have improvements which will make it practically proof against the escape of prisoners. Old brick cell partitions, hinged doors and soft iron bars will give way to an equipment of steel cells with special sanitary arrangements and wash stands in each cell, saw-proof hardened steel bars, sliding doors and an immense steel cage around the entire range of cells, thus penning criminals behind four sets of doors and locks.

New quarters will be provided for the kitchen and laundry and the women's department will be enlarged and isolated from the other corridors.

The new wing will extend in a north-easterly direction from the main corridor to High Street [now Sixth Avenue] *room being left on the latter thoroughfare for the proposed widening by the City. The wing will be 170 feet in length and will give the Jail the shape of a star with a single long point, like a bob-tailed comet. The yard of the Jail will be extended to the extreme limit of the property recently purchased and a high stone wall will be built above Fifth Avenue and High Street.*

The eastern wing will be extended 72 feet and the north wing, which will be occupied by the women prisoners will be constructed 70 feet beyond its present limits. There will be added 390 cells, including 84 cells for women.

At the corner of Fifth Avenue and Ross Street a new turret will be erected to conform with the style of architecture on the south-west angle. The lower floor of the turret will be occupied as an additional ward to the hospital.

Right: Richardson augmented: Osterling's additions to the Jail begun in 1904, copied Richardson's materials and detailing perfectly. The round tower and the visible end of the cell block are by Osterling. The gabled element is by Richardson. Above it is the turret that originally terminated the cell block.

Opposite: Richardson outraged (I): the third major tier of windows was proposed by Osterling to add more space to the Court House. The tower was to be heightened as well.

On June 4, 1904, Osterling appeared before the Grand Jury with his plans and specifications for the Jail. On August 1, the architect signed a contract for the alterations and additions to the Jail *only*. The work on the Jail proceeded according to the contract and specifications with one major exception: the exterior walls of the additions, which were first specified to be of sandstone, were later changed to Milford granite to match the rest of the building. The Jail additions were completed in December 1908 at a total cost of $933,796.37. Although minor interior changes have been made since then, the exterior of the Jail has suffered little amendment: mainly a few alterations and adjustments attendant on the removal of the Hump in 1912-14.

All did not go well with Osterling's scheme to add two stories to the Court House, however. Apparently the architect had convinced the Commissioners as to the value of his idea, but the announcement of the proposed changes provoked protest. On October 13, 1904, the *Gazette* wrote: "Lovers of architecture and beauty were startled yesterday when the announcement was made that two additional stories are to be placed on the Court House. To them it seems like an act of vandalism." *The American Architect* reported nationally: "The architects and intelligent people of Pittsburgh are most unexpectedly called upon to 'save' the Allegheny County Court House, the building which H. H. Richardson fondly regarded as his most successful design." The same magazine a few days later carried the resolution of the Pittsburgh Chapter of the American Institute

of Architects: "Resolved . . . that the contemplated action of the County Commissioners of an addition of several stories to the Allegheny County Court House is hereby condemned and we wish to record our most emphatic protest against it." There was even a popular outcry from local citizens; the *Gazette* reported that "the County Commissioners have received much protest mail."

The best summary of the case against Osterling's scheme is in a pamphlet containing the findings of a committee appointed by the Allegheny County Bar Association:

> *The Committee appointed by this Association at its meeting on the first Friday of November, 1904, to inquire into the contemplated changes to the Court House, respectfully submit the following Report. . . .*
>
> *It seems to your Committee that the questions for consideration are:*
>
> *1. Is the present Court House adequate?*
>
> *2. Ought the people of Allegheny County to try to preserve the Court House as an example of architectural beauty?*
>
> *3. Is the proposed change wise?*
>
> *4. Would not the needs of the county be best subserved by acquiring more ground and erecting new buildings?*
>
> ***(1) IS THE PRESENT COURTHOUSE ADEQUATE?***
>
> *Your Committee is of the opinion that there can be no question upon this. The present Court House is not adequate. The business of the county has increased greatly within the last twenty years and is steadily increasing. . . . Besides, nearly all the present court rooms are not now well adapted to their use, in that they are noisy, poorly ventilated and the acoustic properties bad.*
>
> ***(2) OUGHT THE PEOPLE OF ALLEGHENY COUNTY TO TRY TO PRESERVE THE COURT HOUSE AS AN EXAMPLE OF ARCHITECTURAL BEAUTY?***
>
> *It seems to be universally conceded, both at home and abroad, that the present Court House is a masterpiece of one of the greatest architects of the country, and that Allegheny County possesses in it one of the most perfect examples of architecture to be found in America today. The absolutely correct proportions of the different parts of the building have produced this result. Your Committee feels that this building cannot be changed without destroying its harmony and beauty.*
>
> *However, we have not depended upon our own judgment, but are able to submit to the Association the opinion of those most competent to judge.*
>
> *The Pittsburgh Chapter of the American Institute of Architects considered the question at a meeting, in which they passed a resolution saying, among other things, that:*

"We feel satisfied that any change made on the plans proposed by the published drawings would completely ruin the unity, dignity and proportions of the building."

The International Jury for the Carnegie Institute, composed of ten artists of world-wide reputation, citizens of the United States, Great Britain and France, were so much interested in the question that they voluntarily signed a paper expressing their hope that the authorities would not "allow such an alteration of [the Court House's] *character and design as would be implied in the building of additional stories, an alteration which would, from an artistic point of view, amount to total destruction."*

The Pittsburgh Chapter of American Institute of Architects later appointed a committee to examine in detail into the question, and that committee unanimously reported that "the architectural beauty of the building, which has an international fame as the finest example of modern Romanesque architecture in existence, would be totally destroyed by any attempt to alter its present magnificent proportions."

Mr. F. E. Alden, of Alden & Harlow, who was associated with Mr. Richardson, not only during the building of the Court House but in making the preliminary plans, which extended over several months before the final plans were prepared, says:

"The building, as one of the finest examples of modern architecture in this country, would be completely ruined, not one iota of its present symmetry and beauty remaining; there can be no argument about this." [Similar opinions from other Pittsburgh architects follow.]

None of the architects to whom we wrote, or with whom we talked, except Mr. F. J. Osterling, were of the opinion that the changes could be made without destroying the architectural effect and beauty of the present building. . . .

Your Committee is strongly of the opinion that the people of Allegheny County ought to try to preserve the Court House as an example of architectural beauty.

(3) ***IS THE PROPOSED CHANGE WISE?***

From the standpoint of cost and result, we are of the opinion that the changes proposed would not be wise, in that they are neither practical nor economical. As we understand the plans, it is proposed to remove the present roof and exterior walls of the third story [the present fifth floor] *down to the widow sills, rebuild the exterior walls of the third story and add a fourth and fifth story and new roof. In the interior wall, around the court, it is proposed to build on top of the present wall which now extends to the middle of the second story* [the present third floor]; *so that it means a new interior wall from the middle of the second story and a new exterior wall from the window sills of the third story. It is proposed to remodel materially the interior of the ground and second floors by removing the partitions, the four stairways and elevators, constructing a new stairway in the court, at the center of the Ross Street side of the building, and eight new elevators. A new heating plant is to be put in the attic. The two back towers will be removed, and if the preliminary sketches are followed, the tower in front will have to be torn down to the third story, possibly lower. It is suggested, to meet the architectural requirements of line and proportion, that the tower be rebuilt about thirty feet higher than at present. It is stated that some of the material which will be taken down can be used again in the reconstruction, but it is also stated that the cost of taking down would equal the value of the material which could be used again. . . .*

Mr. Osterling has no detail figures in the way of estimates as to the cost of the new work. He informed us that he had never prepared any specifications nor any detail drawings. He has nothing but preliminary sketches and has two sets of these. . . .

Mr. Osterling's estimate assumes that the present walls and foundations of the Court House are strong enough to carry the additional weight. He assured your committee that he has gone into the matter carefully, and stated that there can be no question that the walls are strong enough.

On the other hand, the committee of architects is of the contrary opinion. They say: "The present walls were built to do the work for which they were designed, and are not of sufficient strength to carry the proposed additional weight. It would be necessary to provide additional foundations and special supports from the foundation up to carry this new work."

Mr. F. E. Alden, who was resident assistant to Mr. Richardson during all the progress of the work, says: "The present walls, piers and foundations are not strong enough to take the proposed additional weight. . . ."

Your Committee has, by the facts submitted to it, been led to the conclusion that the proposed changes would not be wise, and that the cost of doing the work would be altogether out of proportion to the results attained.

Among the reasons suggested to your Committee why this scheme should be adopted, are, first: That the present court rooms are noisy; and second: That it would be inconvenient to have the county offices located in a different building from the court rooms.

Your Committee is of the opinion that there would be no appreciable relief from the noise in the court rooms by putting them on the two higher floors. We believe that the noises from the street, especially if the Court House is surrounded by high buildings, will be fully as great at the higher elevation. In this we are supported by the judgment of competent architects. . . .

We think that this building should be kept for the courts and the offices essential to the courts, and that it is ample for this. The rooms are splendidly lighted. There are four rooms on the third floor, particularly well adapted for court rooms, one of which is now used by the Supreme Court; and there are others which are well adapted for that purpose. We do not think that this Association would hesitate to give up its beautiful room, if necessary, and take a room on another floor.

It is evident that some of the difficulty in hearing in the court rooms is caused by the ceilings being too high, and that this could be largely remedied, at a small expense, by putting in false ceilings and thus decreasing the height of the rooms. We believe that the disturbance from street noises can be almost entirely removed by keeping the windows shut and by installing an adequate modern ventilating apparatus in the Court House. We are assured by architects that this can be done.

(4) ***WOULD NOT THE NEEDS OF THE COUNTY BE BEST SUBSERVED BY ACQUIRING NEW GROUND AND ERECTING NEW BUILDINGS? . . .***

We believe it is a mistake to get a public building too large, and to try and keep everything in a great county, such as this, under one roof, for the reason that it requires such an immense building as to produce congestion in the elevators and corridors, and to make it very difficult for one not accustomed to visiting it to find the particular office which he desires. We think this is demonstrated by comparing the public buildings in the two great cities of New York and Philadelphia. In New York they are separated, and in Philadelphia they are all collected under one roof. We believe the New York system is the better.

We think there can be no doubt about the proposition, that the county offices can be much more conveniently arranged, and better facilities provided for the transaction of business therein, in a building or buildings specially designed for the purpose than they can be in a building the primary design of which is the accommodation of courts. . . .

Your Committee is of the opinion that the County Commissioners ought not to hesitate to acquire additional land in the neighborhood of the Court House, with the idea of meeting the wants of the public business by the erection of new buildings as they are required. There is no reason to doubt that if the county should acquire real estate in the neighborhood of the Court House, and borrowed the money for the purpose, the enhancement in value would save it from any loss. We recommend the purchase of all the rest of the square bounded by Ross, Diamond, Grant Streets, and Fourth Avenue. . . . The county would then have abundance of room for an additional building or

> *buildings to meet the needs of the public service as they arise. Such building or buildings might be made economical in construction, efficient in use and architectural ornaments to the city. . . .*
>
> *To recapitulate, the conclusions that we have reached are as follows:*
>
> *(1) That the proposed alterations of the Court House would amount to the destruction of the architectural beauty of the present building.*
>
> *(2) That the cost of procuring the additional room in the method prescribed would be excessive and uneconomical.*
>
> *(3) That the public convenience would be better subserved by building a separate building or buildings to take care of the offices which are not essential to the transaction of the business of the courts.*

The storm of public protest and this well-written pamphlet convinced the Commissioners that Osterling's proposal should not be accepted.

Shortly before, the Pittsburgh Chapter of the American Institute of Architects had issued a report containing a design for the area contiguous to the Court House; a public square would display to good advantage the north elevation of the Court House. A year later the final scheme was published in a Pittsburgh periodical, *Construction.* A map published with the article shows a symmetrical, axial Beaux-Arts plan imposed on the jumbled terrain of the area north of the Court House. The rugged topography of Pittsburgh has never been kind to Neo-Baroque city planning, and nothing came of the proposed public square.

In 1906, the Commissioners of Allegheny County encouraged the City of Pittsburgh to replace its aging and overcrowded building at Smithfield Street and Oliver Avenue by taking over the Court House as a city hall. As reported in *Construction:*

> *The plan of the County Commissioners is to use the money received from the City in purchasing more property in the square bounded by Ross, Diamond, and Grant Streets and Fourth Avenue and the erection on this square of a magnificent County building, adequate for all future needs. The matter has been discussed at some length, but the City officials and many prominent citizens of both Pittsburgh and Allegheny do not see their way clear to give assent to the project. While the present Court House would undoubtedly make a magnificent City Hall, yet it is the opinion generally expressed that the price asked—six million dollars—is too high and more than the City should pay.*

The City official Edward Manning Bigelow was reported to have said that the County should give the Court House to the City, because it was mostly the taxes of Pittsburgh and Allegheny that had paid for it. He did not think, however, that the Court House could be adapted as a city hall. This proposal, too, was disregarded.

The Pittsburgh architect John T. Comes stated in an article published in 1906 that the defeat of the Osterling scheme of 1904 by no means implied that the threat to the Court House by injudicious alterations and additions was no longer extant. This prognostication was speedily borne out by the publication in 1907 of the most horrendous scheme ever brought forward for the expansion of the Court House. This nightmarish proposal was the brainchild of the highly-talented architect Henry Hornbostel, who had publicly stated during the height of the Osterling controversy, "A shot gun should be used on anyone who would mar the Allegheny County building by adding two stories to it . . . the building is too perfect to tamper with." His memory proved short; Hornbostel attempted to mar Richardson's perfection by adding a *multitude* of stories.

The American Architect reported the scheme:

> *Palmer and Hornbostel, New York and Pittsburgh, and Maurice Trimble, Pittsburgh, have designed and submitted to the County Commissioners a plan for a large addition to the Allegheny County Court House. The design consists of a massive tower 90 x 90 feet by 700 feet high, to cost about $2,000,000 to be constructed of skeleton steel frame and granite, the structure to be erected in the area way* [courtyard] *of the Court House. The Commissioners are considering the design. The tower is designed to carry out the present architectural scheme of the Court House.*

The American Architect again reported on the scheme a few days later—but not favorably. *Inland Architect* illustrated the architects' perspective drawing but made no comment. The Pittsburgh *Builder* penned a satirical article on the tower scheme. If the Osterling scheme was unacceptable this was even more so, and if the Commissioners did consider the design they did not do so seriously. The Hornbostel proposal soon met the oblivion it deserved. This monster tower illustrated the degree to which the highrise megalomania had become entrenched in the early twentieth century. It is possible that Hornbostel, who had a flair for drama, may have considered his project a glorious "stunt" or an outrageous "attention-getter." So far as is known the Commissioners did not entertain any more proposals for altering the Court House. The only feasible solution to the problem of limited space was to build a new building. The Commissioners continued to buy parcels of land in the long block south of the Court House.

Attention next focused on the issue of making one final cut in the slope of Grant's Hill. The Commissioners' *Minutes* record that on October 27, 1911 "an agreement was made between the County of Allegheny and the City of Pittsburgh for grading streets and alleys and highways in the Hump District." The Hump was finally removed in 1912 and 1913. The new grades meant that all the elevations of the Court House and Jail had to conform to lowered street levels. On the north and south elevations

Richardson outraged (II): Henry Hornbostel's project of 1907.

Left: Richardson en fête: *this incredible dressing-up of the Court House courtyard, including a board floor and steel roof trusses, was done for a meeting of the Tancred Commandery of the Knights of Templar in 1898.*

Below: lowering the Hump in 1913.

The Ross Street doorway of the Jail after the lowering of the Hump.

of the Court House the change in level was met by interpolating raised, narrow granite terraces between the walls of the building and the sidewalk. On Ross Street the entrances to both the Court House and Jail were elongated downward and flights of steps were lengthened to meet the old first-floor levels. The exposed foundation walls (the cut was not particularly deep here) were encased in granite. At Grant and Fifth the cut was especially marked, resulting in a change of some 16 feet in the street level. The Grant Street front of the Court House, its foundation walls exposed even further, also had to have a new granite terrace approached by steps on either side, so that the main entrance arches could be reached.

On February 20, 1913, the Commissioners' *Minutes* recorded that "the Commissioners awarded to and signed a contract with Alden and Harlow of Pittsburgh . . . for preparing plans, details and specifications for altering the Court House and Jail buildings to conform to the Hump cut."

The Grant Street front of the Court House was the most changed by the removal of the Hump. The grand and mysterious effect of entering the low, cavernous Syrian arches of the portals directly from the street was gone. However, the strange disdainful Byzantine lions on either side of the entry could still be consulted close at hand; something was retained of Richardson's primal majesty of approach. So it was to remain until Grant Street was widened in 1927.

Left: the Ross Street front of the Court House after the lowering of the Hump.

Below: the County Buildings around 1915, with the site for the City-County Building in preparation. New steps and terraces surround the Court House, rising from the new street level. The Grant Street entrances are still at the original level, reached by a Romanesque terrace by Alden & Harlow. Street widening would remove this in 1927.

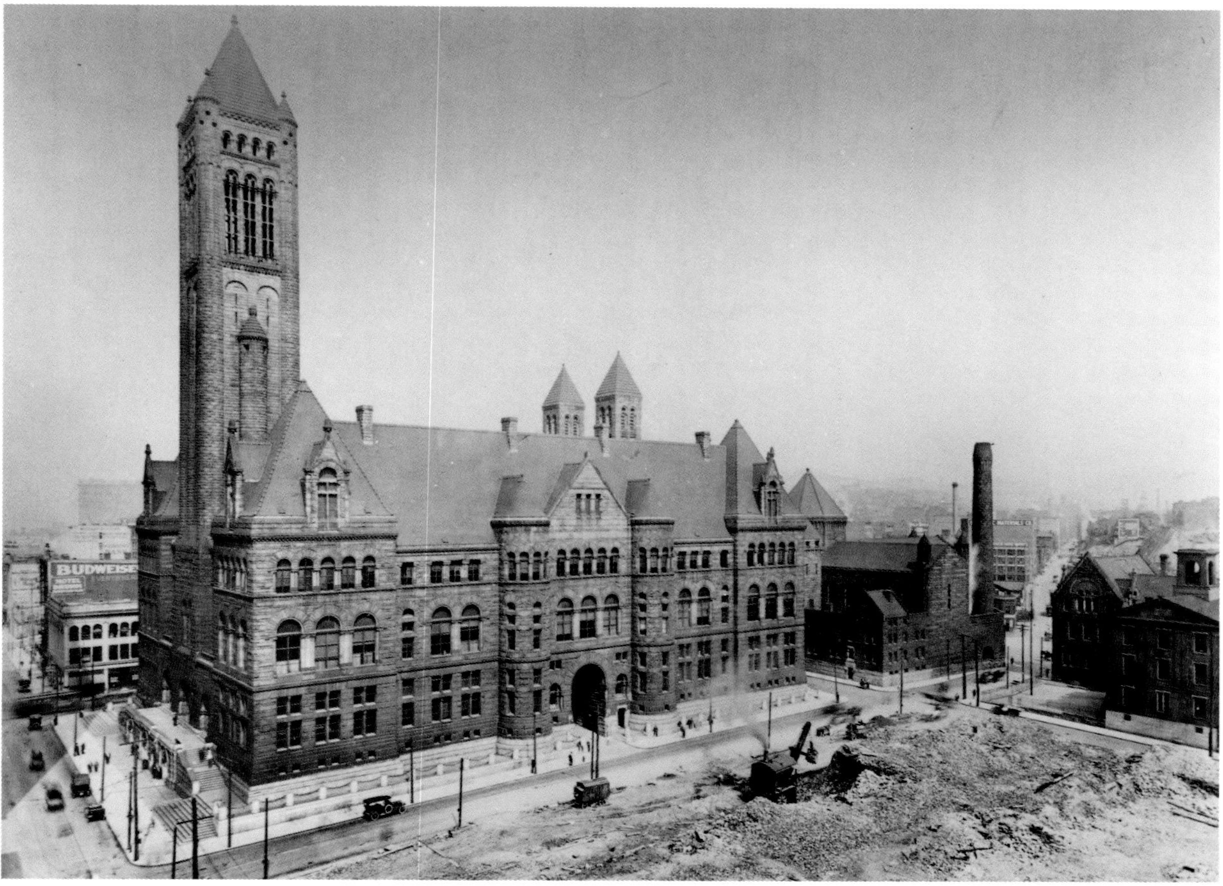

The City-County Building, completed 1917. Although Edward B. Lee and Palmer, Hornbostel & Jones are given as associated architects, the boldness and verve of the conception suggest the mind of Henry Hornbostel. This is basically an office building, a box of small spaces with no room for Romantic skyline features, yet in its own ways it echoes the Court House: a granite exterior, three prominent archways on Grant Street, one on Ross. The archways are connected by an airy, dramatic corridor through the interior light court.

THE TOWER AND THE CITY

1914-70

While the Hump was being removed, the County Commissioners were implementing the projected plan to build a Court House annex in the lot south of Diamond Street, which was now the County's possession. Since the City of Pittsburgh also needed a new city hall, there was a growing sentiment among City and County officials to construct a monumental building that could be useful to both parties. The competition was restricted to architects of Allegheny County. Cass Gilbert of New York was selected as consulting architect to the building committee to prepare specifications for the competition.

The competition took place in 1913, and early in 1914 the results were published in *Architecture* and *Architectural Review*. Edward B. Lee, a Pittsburgher, was awarded the contract for what was later called the City-County Building. With him was associated the firm of Palmer, Hornbostel and Jones, with offices in Pittsburgh and New York. All the published designs were in a Classical style (there was no question of reviving the Romanesque manner of Richardson), and their basic form was that of a severe rectangle of about eight or nine stories; the projects both of Janssen and Abbott and R. M. Trimble display central ornamental towers.

In October 1916, the Pittsburgh *Builder* published a selection of the revised drawings for the City-County Building, incorporating all changes from the competition drawings. Comparison of the early and final versions reveals an extensive stripping on the exterior of the elaborate grammar of Classical ornament, so apparent as part of the winning design. The revision is a tribute to the all-pervading rigor and severity of Pittsburgh's architectural tone. Granite was chosen for the exterior walls, and brick and terra cotta for the courtyard. Although the granite for the City-County Building was smoothly dressed in keeping with its Classical style, the intention to honor the material of the Court House is obvious.

The second version of the Grant Street elevation rises to a solemn pitch of Neo-Classical grandeur. The three great arches of the entrance loggia straitly prepare the way for the domed vaults of Guastavino tiles that speak of Rome and Persia, and yet remain, however eclectically and exotically, authentically Pittsburgh. If the entrance to the Court House in its original lowering form was something close and mysterious, the City-County Building provides an amplitude of opening that is almost superfluous, and yet somehow bleakly just. In the plane of the facade above the loggia, the recessed Doric colonnade with its range of rugged fluted columns resembles the monumental Greek portico of Chislett's Court House.

The side elevations of the City-County Building on both Forbes Avenue and Fourth Avenue are of an almost brutal simplicity worthy of the Neo-Classicists of the Age of Reason: rationalism could hardly go farther. Here, Classicism is so reduced to its simplest terms that there appear to be no terms at all. The square windows of the lower floors seem to have been punched out of the granite walls. The self-effacing severity of the Forbes Avenue elevation is a lively contrast to the equally masculine, equally rugged, south facade of the Court House. Richardson's wall, despite its basic simplicity, is full of movement; intricate, dense with protrusions of form and recessions of shadow. There are small coruscations of surface, hints in the ordered complexity of infinite textures, forms, spaces—all subsumed under the solid and pervasive mass. The massive simplicity of the south elevation of the City-County Building seems like a neutral backdrop to the complexity of the Court House.

Perhaps the best physical description of it is found in a guide book published in Pittsburgh in 1916:

> *The new City and County Building, now in course of erection, will attract attention. . . . The dimensions are 184 feet by 306 feet. There are nine stories and three mezzanine stories. The plan is rectangular, built around a hollow court, 144 feet by 84 feet. The height of the building from the curb to the main cornice is 151 feet. . . .*
>
> *The offices in the new building are provided on the basis that the City's business can be conducted in these offices until the City is twice as large as it is now. After which time it being the further intention that either the City or the County will relinquish its space in the building and turn it over to the remaining party; if it should be the City of Pittsburgh, it is estimated that the City can conduct its business in this building until it is more than four times as large as it is now.*

Neither the County nor the City has, however, relinquished its portion of the building; although some changes have been made, both parties still occupy the structure jointly.

In May 1919, the Pittsburgh *Builder*, as a kind of climax to its career (it ceased publication shortly after), published a large group of excellent photographs of the completed building. Of these, some of the interiors are especially interesting. The Supreme Court Room, the Law Library, and the Council Chamber are simply treated, but still are monumental in the Classical tradition; they are an interesting contrast to the interiors of the Court House. (Incidentally, the old Law Library in the Court House had by this time been divided up into smaller offices; its magnificent approach at the top of the great staircase of the Court House now led to a cluttered warren of rooms.)

On February 29, 1916, the Commissioners' *Minutes* record that

a letter was received which recommended that Alden and Harlow be selected as architects in connection with alterations to the Court House and Jail, necessitated by the widening of Diamond Street and the changes in the use of the Court House when the new County and Municipal Building is complete.

On November 4, 1921 the *Minutes* record

a letter from the County Engineer in which he calls attention to the introduction of an ordinance in council [of the City of Pittsburgh] *widening Grant Street from Water Street to Seventh Avenue, which if passed will require the removal of the present steps leading up to the first floor of the Court House.*

In 1923-25 the Alden and Harlow plans were implemented to the degree that changes were made in the great entrance arches between the courtyard and Fifth Avenue and Diamond Street (now Forbes Avenue). This was the only major alteration to the Court House from 1914 until the reworking of the Grant Street front in 1927-28. The upper part of the archway in each entrance was enclosed, thus bringing the recessed wall

Left: a side of the Court House as sketched in 1924. The archway was unenclosed originally, though the first-floor corridor, on the courtyard side, passed through it in a sort of covered bridge.

Below: a side archway today, as enclosed in the mid-1920s. An original arch bearing the first-floor corridor appears on the far side of the courtyard.

of the second floor out almost to the plane of both the Fifth Avenue and Diamond Street walls. This left a low driveway giving access to the court, and it is interesting that the low segmental vaults of these driveways were roofed with Guastavino tiles. These changes reduced the dramatic impact of these tall arches, but not sufficiently to harm Richardson's original conception.

The most important changes in the exterior of the Court House during the 1920s were those made in connection with the widening of Grant Street to a width of 80 feet in 1926-29. These alterations on the Grant Street elevation were extensive, involving the removal of the Alden and Harlow terrace and changing the basement floor to serve as the main entrance to the building with access to the great stair hall by means of a double interior staircase near the front wall. To achieve this result, the portals were made into windows and their exterior arches were elongated so that doors could be introduced below. This solution had already been considered at the time of the removal of the Hump, and it did the least damage to Richardson's original conception.

The work of altering the Court House began in 1928. The interior hallways in the basement were still unfinished in the early part of 1929, as witness an entry in the Commissioners' *Minutes* for April 11, 1929 relative to the awarding of the contract for electric fixtures. The new entrance corridors in the basement were vaulted with Guastavino tiles.

The alterations of Stanley Roush, the County Architect, to the Grant Street elevation are discreet, graceful, and imbued with a vast respect for the Richardsonian fabric. His carved ornamental detail—the friezes of birds and animals done in the suave, archaeological manner of the Romanesque Revival of the 1920s—forms an interesting contrast with that of the original Evans carvers and with the handsome lions guarding the original portals, which were removed from the street activity by the elongation of their pedestals.

A humorous note in regard to the inner courtyard of the building is recorded in the Commissioners' *Minutes* on September 30, 1930:

> *A resolution relative to clearing out the Court House yard and making it safe for pedestrians, and to discontinue the dumping of contraband liquors, moonshine, and other confiscated concoctions, in the yard, was read, and a copy ordered sent to the superintendent of buildings.*

The courtyard escaped yet another scheme of the early 1920s to build an addition to the existing structure. The Pittsburgh *Post* of September 7, 1922 reported discussion of a plan to make a wing connecting the north and south sides of the Court House through the center of the court; the result would be two light courts instead of one. "Colonel Eric Fisher Wood asserted that the new building would not change the outer appearance of the Court House." In an article in the Pittsburgh *Sun* for September 12, 1922, it was stated that "working drawings were being prepared for the

Left: a detail of the stonework.

Left, below: the Samuel Yellin grillework.

Below: Stanley Lawson Roush, the County Architect, inserted these blandly tasteful doorways when the Grant Street entrances were moved to street level in the late 1920s.

new wing by Rutan, Russell, and Wood.'' However, on October 31, 1922 the Commissioners' *Minutes* reported:

> *Mr. Cain moved . . . that on account of the Judges having refused their approval of the proposed addition to the Court House that Rutan, Russell and Wood be notified to work on plans for said addition until they are inked, rendering their bill for the work up to that point.*

That was essentially the end of the project, and the courtyard retained—and has continued to retain—its original form.

The first serious threat to the existence of the Jail was proposed in the mid-1920s. William S. Huff, a young Pittsburgh architect, admirably told the story in 1958 in an essay, ''Richardson's Jail'':

> [I]*n 1924 a very great danger to the Jail developed and lasted at least six years. It threatened either to remove the Jail altogether or to emasculate it so thoroughly that the value of the remains would be slight indeed.*
>
> *As reported in the* Post-Gazette *in 1927, ''The County Planning Commission recommended the removal of the jail October 3, 1924, and on March 6, 1925, approved a plan presented to place the jail on the upper floors of the county building proposed to be built at Diamond and Ross Streets for which $1,000,000 was authorized in the people's bond issue of April, 1924.'' And the* Gazette Times *had previously revealed in March, 1925, that the Commissioners planned a skyscraper jail, a 17 story combination office and prison building to be erected at Diamond and Ross Streets and Fourth Avenue, while the existing Jail site, bounded by Fifth, Sixth, Ross, and Diamond, was to be developed into a ''spacious traffic square around which all vehicles could rotate and its interior could be developed as a suitable park, which would prove a great convenience and comfort.''*
>
> *Another* Gazette Times *news item was headlined in 1926, ''Virtually Assure Removal of Jail from Present Site.'' ''For more than a year the project of removing the present jail was steered through a stormy course against the opposition of citizens and organizations who objected to even partial destruction of the architectural 'masterpiece' consisting of the court house and jail, connected by the 'bridge of sighs' over Grant Street. What had become of the project was the subject of many inquiries, nothing having been heard of it for months.''*
>
> *The principal ''opposition'' came from the Pittsburgh Chapter of the American Institute of Architects which had not taken a position against ''even partial destruction'' but which had formulated in October, 1925, recommendations, ''proposing to reduce the structure to its original extent and exterior condition and to remodel the*

The A.I.A. project to save the Jail in the late 1920s. The Osterling additions are shown removed, but so are Richardson's outer wall and chimney.

interior to serve as a hall of records, with a view to conserving it to future generations.'' The AIA proposal, which possibly grew out of an earlier suggestion by County Architect Stanley L. Roush, called for the removal of the parts of the building that were added in 1905 with the claim by the AIA that its ''conception of the proposed hall was taken from existing drawings of the original jail and a floor plan found in records of Richardson's Works.''

Whether by inference or actual misinformation, the great wall has, as a result of this proposal, been identified with those additions of 1905; and the facts have since become so confused that many Pittsburghers today support the belief that the original Jail of Richardson had never possessed a wall at all. The responsibility for this erroneous belief can be traced to [an] *ambiguously worded AIA Recommendation*[:] *''To restore the Jail building to Richardson's original design will necessitate the removal of the forbidding looking walls of the jail yard, the diagonal north-east wing, parts of the north wing and east wing, and, perhaps, some other minor portions.''*

To accomplish the reduction of the building to its original proportions required, to be sure, the ''removal of the forbidding looking walls,'' for the simple reason that, when the building was expanded, the original Richardson walls had to be moved outward and enlarged.

But this is not to say that these walls were not of the exact design and intent of Richardson or that their construction was not executed in precisely the same manner as the Jail yard walls erected in 1885-86. . . . To those of perception even this evidence would be unnecessary, for a single glance at the wall itself reveals at once the Master's design. Furthermore, it may confidently be asserted that those sections which are additions have happily been executed with remarkable sympathy for Richardson's original concept and detail. It seems most probable that these additions were the design of aforementioned architect Osterling; and, if this be so, history has smiled upon the Richardson buildings, wherein the Court House was spared the outrage of the proposed upper story additions while the Jail was expanded in a most intelligent manner. To be sure, additions change, but they do not always destroy—they sometimes add. In this case, the extension of two cell blocks was most logical; and the addition of the fourth, on the 45 degree, most successfully carried through the daring dynamics of Richardson's original scheme.

The AIA plan was publicized widely by the City papers, Charette [the local architectural magazine], *and by the Pittsburgh periodical* Progress, *which in its May 1930 issue enlarged upon these recommendations of dubious merit. It was the opinion of* Progress *that the "Forbidding Aspect Should Be Eliminated."*

"The high and ominous enclosing walls, and the huge and gloomy bulk of the various wings, are characteristics which may be said to be particularly depressing. There is no doubt that these characteristics are psychological obstacles to a normal use of the private properties on the north side of Fifth Avenue and thereby retard their economic success. . . . [F]*or the relief of the private properties just mentioned, it is desirable to demolish at least the Jail walls, the north end of the Ross Street wing, all of the large diagonal wing and part of the east wing."*

The popular AIA recommendations were espoused by a large number of civic groups and were discussed at a special meeting of the Chamber of Commerce in January, 1928, where even Pittsburgh architect Edward J. Weber apparently submitted to the plan in an attempt to save at least "half the hog," though earlier he had made an eloquent and enlightened appeal for the building in toto. *He recognized the Jail, the Court House, and the connecting Bridge of Sighs as an inseparable group and pleaded against the desecration of any one of the units of the Court House complex; "Turn the whole into a public museum," he begged. A great portion of this article, printed in the* Pittsburgh Sunday Post *of March 29, 1925, I am impelled to recall here due to its penetrating insight into the quality of this great building, including a deep understanding of the Jail's most powerful external feature—the controversial wall. . . .*

Opposite: a close view of the Jail masonry.

> *''Some will object that the jail is mostly wall. To be sure, part of it is a plain wall, but what a wall! A beautiful wall, beautiful to the extreme. Those walls suggest strength, and those frowning towers are so calm and magnificent in their austerity. Examine the graduation of the stone courses. From great width at the bottom to narrow courses at the top where less strength is required.*
>
> *''Observe the artistic proportion of each stone; with what nicety the lengths are varied in proportion, of from one by two to one by seven; then, the refinement of the curve of the ovolo moulding forming the water table. How beautifully battered* [inclined] *the wall is! See how clearly the plain east wall is broken and handsomely silhouetted by the gable—with its twin pinnacles—of one of the prison wings.*
>
> *''If there is no beauty in the side elevations of the towers of 'Notre Dame de Paris,' then I'll grant there is none in the Allegheny County prison. If there is no beauty in the Palazzo Strozzi, then the prison is without the quality of great architecture. If the Pitti Palace is monstrous, then I'll admit so, too, is the prison. . . .*
>
> *''Truly, kind reader, ours is the most beautiful prison building in the world today and this fact is incontrovertible.*
>
> *''Here is a smoke stack. What an utilitarian thing is a smoke stack! Yet, it is in this case not an eyesore, as nearly all smoke stacks are. The artist has made of it a thing of delight. . . .*
>
> *''Too much praise it is not possible to bestow on the prison portion of the court house group, truly a most interesting work of art, for which one will have to travel far to see the equal of in any type of building.''*
>
> *However, these voices faded; the plans of both the AIA and the Commissioners were laid aside. The new County Office Building was built during 1930 without its skyscraper prison, but the steel was so designed that it might at some future date see such a project through to realization.*

The high-rise that figured so prominently in the Jail controversy was Stanley Roush's County Office Building, erected in 1929-31 at the corner of Diamond Street (now Forbes Avenue) and Ross Street. This, the only corner of the intersection not occupied by County structures, was the site of this last addition to the complex of Allegheny County buildings.

The building is encased in limestone, but the great three-story arcades of the lower section have columns of polished granite that discreetly allude to the fashionable Romanesque and ''Spanish'' ornamental detailing of the 1920s. Despite this sense of amenity and grace in the lower stories one is conscious of a separation here between the overly-monumental base and the ''sensed'' stories that were never added. In its dense, squat way the City-County Building is at least ''complete''—as a composition it exists as a whole. The County Office Building, in contrast, seems tentative, ''chopped off.'' And yet even so truncated, the building literally has ''style''—and who today would be so archaeological as to undertake its finishment?

Stanley Roush was stylistically a child of his time; the Romanesque high-rise manner, so persuasively and gracefully advanced by Arthur Loomis Harmon in his Shelton Hotel of 1922-23 in New York, had become ubiquitous by the end of the 1920s. If Roush, in adopting the Harmon formula for his building and in attempting to give the new manner a Richardsonian monumentality, has not really ''brought off' the amalgamation, he has at least not created anything antipathetic.

All the architects who added to the County complex were acolytes at the elder altar of genius; they created handsome ''settings,'' ''surroundings,'' but the Court House and Jail are still the lions, the enduring pride of the city. Their eminence has always been so just and unquestionable that they have survived all assaults. When one considers what might have happened to them, they have been treated very gently.

The County Office Building, by Stanley Lawson Roush. The style, Italian Romanesque with a touch of Art Deco, responds politely to the style of the County Buildings, while the tall arcades are in scale with the huge archway of the City-County Building directly across Ross Street.

During the 1930s and '40s few changes were made to the Court House and the Jail. Time—and Pittsburgh atmosphere—had darkened the buildings to the point where it was necessary to have the Court House and Jail cleaned in 1934. The cleaning process was successful, and for a time the pinkish granite could almost be seen in its pristine state.

In 1934, the Pittsburgh artist Vincent Nesbert (1899-1976) was commissioned to create a mural for the lobby of the great hall stair. According to the Commissioners' *Minutes* for March 27, 1934:

> *A letter was read from John O'Connor, Junior Secretary of the Regional Committee, Public Works of Art, Washington, D.C. relative to art projects being handled through the P.W.A. and advising that Vincent Nesbert, a well trained and competent artist of Pittsburgh, one of the fine artists employed by the Regional Committee was assigned the problem of making studies for a mural "Justice" which might be placed on the Grant Street wall on the main floor of the Court House, and his salary will be paid by the Public Works of Art Projects.*

Nesbert painted two more murals in 1935, *Peace* and *Prosperity* for the side walls of the lobby, and in 1938 two others, *The Battle of Grant's Hill* and *Fort Pitt.*

Again in 1954 another serious threat to the existence of the Jail is recorded in "Richardson's Jail" by William S. Huff:

> *On October 6 and 7, 1954, the Pittsburgh newspapers reported that Conrad Hilton was considering the Jail property as a possible hotel site. The County officials leapt at the opportunity to voice their opinion that the Jail was a deterrent to progress and of no aesthetic value, nor did they leave any doubt that they would deliver the Jail with swiftest alacrity to the hands of the man with the right price. Though a small group of Pittsburghers as quickly rallied to the cause of preserving the Jail (along with a vision toward an Industrial Museum), the newspapers generally made light of the "Friends of the Ross Street Prison" in threatening their efforts as eccentric delusions of the lunatic fringe to save some "grisly old structure." The* Pittsburgh Post-Gazette *presumed to pose as an arbiter of American culture, while disregarding the authority of the architectural historians, when it editorialized on at least two occasions:*
>
> *"The architecture of the Allegheny County jail would be more appropriate to the old section of Nuremberg than to a modern American city like Pittsburgh. This gloomy stone pile has long contributed to the medieval appearance of the upper area of the Triangle, which is at odds with the general urban redevelopment program.*
>
> *"Thus County Commissioner John Kane's hint that someone is interested in replacing the jail with a modern structure, perhaps a hotel is welcome. Such a move would contribute to the redevelopment*

Opposite: the original Court House entrance lobby around 1970 with Vincent Nesbert's murals of the 1930s. The stair from the new Grant Street entrance has a Roush replica of Richardson's balustrade detailing and stair lamps.

of the long neglected commercial area east of Grant Street. We hope it will be done. . . .

''Removal of the jail from its present site impresses us as a good idea because the building is singularly unattractive, because a jail, being tax-exempt property, should be on relatively inexpensive outlying land, and because this development would offer the dual opportunity to improve the street pattern and put the improved property on the city's tax books.

As indicated by the Post-Gazette *editorials, many wish the Jail site developed commercially; there is the desire to return this land to the tax books. Yet, it is inconceivable that a city which possesses the potential wealth of Pittsburgh cannot allow space to this singular masterpiece. Of course, it has frequently been noted that the great monuments of Europe have most often been spared by the dubious fortune of bankruptcy. But if the increasing hordes of Americans continue to flock to Europe each summer on the affectation of inspecting its art treasures, the Europeans will themselves presently be in a position to afford the replacement of these burdensome monuments and land-consuming ruins with spanking modern commercial ventures in reflection of the American propensity to dispose of its unproductive landmarks. Poor, indeed, we are—culturally, as well as economically—if we can no longer afford this building in our midst.*

Traffic engineers claim there is a traffic problem here. This building, they say, creates a bottleneck. Yet the streets here are no narrower than in the rest of the city (though one sidewalk, I admit, is lacking); therefore, it would be naive to believe the city's traffic ills would be solved by widening Diamond (now Forbes), Fifth Avenue, or Sixth Avenue at this point. And a commercial development could only add to congestion here; by its very nature it would be a traffic generator. No! Good city planners are, in fact, trained to find solutions that will not only make use of physical endowments, but also put to advantage the cultural heritage. Shall Pittsburgh scrape away its hills and fill in its valleys for lack of imagination in traffic engineering? Led by enlightened planners with the cooperation of Federal, State, and private civic groups, our sister city, Philadelphia, not only has cleared a mall before Independence Hall; but in this same area it is rehabilitating the crumbling masterpieces of William Strickland, an early [19th]*-century master. For Philadelphians, being privileged to possess these treasures, have realized the responsibilities they bear the Nation as custodians of an American culture. But in Pittsburgh, we honor alone our Block House—and this only after the long hard fight by a small but aroused and determined citizenry which was aware of what we possessed.*

But possibly the most difficult challenge, if not the most annoying of circumstances, is the absurd necessity to defend a building which belongs to a period of architecture that is presently suffering unjustified abuse. Our age seems bent on discrediting the Victorian Era much in the same manner the Renaissance discredited the great achievements of the later medieval period and bestowed the derogatory title of "Gothic" (inferring barbarism) upon that era. It required centuries to right this wrong and to restore those great works to the proper place of respect in Man's cultural history—but only after many of the monuments had been lost or defaced. Is the "Pittsburgh Renaissance" any the wiser for it?

Sociological and penological developments of the past century have made the Jail obsolete, and understandably the Commissioners and Board of Prison Inspectors are ever ready to rid themselves of it. The greatest deterrent thus far seems to have been the sheer bulk which assures an expensive undertaking to any entrepreneur who plans to tear apart. Mr. Hilton has since found his hotel site, and the Jail is again returned to that limbo between promises of preservation and threats of demolition. Apparently the County commissioners have innocently provided a shrewd business man with a convenient ruse. But the next time we may not be so fortunate; for we may awaken one morning to discover that the Commissioners, wishing to avoid another public storm, have quietly exercised their invested powers (neglecting a moral obligation) and sold irrevocably the Jail to a more serious bidder. The real threat to the Jail has not been Mr. Hilton; the danger still exists as long as persons in authority find no place in their program for the preservation of this outstanding monument.

Although the local group of preservationists received support from many prominent architects and architectural historians throughout the country, and another local newspaper, the *Sun Telegraph*, supported their position, the Pittsburgh Chapter of the American Institute of Architects, at a meeting on November 16, 1954, refused to support the movement to preserve the Jail for fear of going on record as standing in the way of "Pittsburgh's Progress." This was indeed a lamentable descent from the position that they had taken in 1904 and 1925. However, as William Huff notes,

in 1956 the Architectural Record, *in honor of the AIA centennial celebration, composed a panel of fifty architects and scholars, to select America's fifty "most significant buildings" of the past one hundred years. The Allegheny County buildings tied for seventeenth place, and only this and one other building represented the achievements in the field of governmental buildings.*

After much work on the part of the preservationists the threat to the Jail was dissipated, but one still wonders if this was not because Conrad Hilton found a better site for his Pittsburgh hotel. In 1957, while the preservation fight no longer seemed so critical, the exterior of the Court House was cleaned again, but not the Jail. Those people concerned with the Jail's preservation considered this ominous; however, the Jail was cleaned in 1963.

Numerous changes had been made in the interior of the Court House since 1914. The most recent change was in lowering the ceilings of several of the courtrooms. On August 14, 1970, the Pittsburgh *Post-Gazette* reported:

> *Seven court rooms on the third floor...and one on the fifth are undergoing such surgery as the lowering of the twenty-four foot ceilings to twelve feet, four inches. And new wiring, air conditioning and lighting.*
>
> *Ancient oak paneling, as old as the building, is blooming again as the grime encrusted old varnish is scraped off....*
>
> *The lower portions of the windows in the massive old rooms will be retained but the arched tops have been painted black to keep out heat from the sun. They will disappear as ceilings are lowered and will be covered with non-acoustical half-inch board.*

One cannot object to the introduction of modern amenities and conveniences into the great rooms, but it is unfortunate that the spatial concept of Richardson's courtrooms has been so drastically altered.

But it is to the great tower of the building that we always return and with it I shall complete my chronicle of the building's rise and continuation.

Secular towers of the Middle Ages and the Renaissance were intended to house a bell or bells. The first Allegheny County Court House had a bell, and when that building was abandoned, the bell (with its "cracked and crazy voice") was moved to the new jail on Grant's Hill.

One of Richardson's early studies for the Court House tower featured a clock; if there had been a clock, there also would have had to have been a bell to sound the hour. However, the clock was never placed in the tower, and since it was not believed necessary for the Court House to have a bell, no bell was ever placed in the belfry.

Nor was any ever placed there but in 1966-67 a 183-"bell" carillon was installed in the tower in memory of all the war dead of Allegheny County. However, it is bell-less: as the *Pittsburgh Press* stated on January 19, 1967, "The instrument consists of miniature bell units made of bronze bell metal. When struck by metal hammers these produce true bell tones which are amplified a million times, giving the same sound as massive traditional cast bells. It will make the same sound as fifty tons of bells." It was dedicated on June 20, 1967. Finally the tower found a voice.

The tower is still an integral part of the city. It is seen, and like its great prototypes, now has a voice of its own. But it is not really necessary for it to sing. Its very presence is enough. Of all the towers of the city, the Court House tower is still the most magnificent, the best beloved. As its creator was aware, it *is* the city.

THE TOWER AND THE CITY SINCE 1970

by Walter C. Kidney

Over the years, almost every large building undergoes alterations to keep it suited to its roles as a working structure. In the process, such architectural grandeur as it possesses is likely to be compromised or endangered. The decorative work requires repair, but often the cheapest way to "repair" it is to get rid of it. The entrance hall looks impressive, but more office or storage space is needed and there are other (though humbler) ways of entering and leaving. Aesthetics and pride are in competition with utility and economy.

Richardson's original plans for the Court House and the Jail were lucid and carefully composed; perhaps the only major inherent vice was the heating and ventilation problem built into the cell-block arrangement. But the increase of County business, accommodated only temporarily by the construction of the City-County Building, has made for many changes in both the Court House and the Jail. So have standards of use that differ from those of the 1880s. The poetry of the grand staircase and the outer wall of the Jail have remained basically unharmed, but the prose of the offices and courtrooms has been re-edited many times, losing something in the process. New partitions have been raised, and ceilings dropped. Architecturally this is not very satisfactory, even though it represents no major loss.

During the 1970s, a number of more important changes occurred. Perhaps we should discuss first the uneasy, inconclusive, continuing question of what is going to happen to the Jail. The Jail's reputation as a place of confinement had been wavering, though sometimes it was hard to know how much objective information the public was getting. The warden in the early 1970s, William Robinson, received an excellent press as a humane and imaginative administrator in charge of a facility that had been bad but was rapidly getting better. But the coverage began to be less than perfectly favorable even before Robinson left in 1975, and most of the stories of the Jail since that time were of rats and roaches comming up from the old canal tunnel near by, of homosexual rape, graft, and bad food, and of the notorious detention room, where violent prisoners were strapped to cots for days at a time. In mid-1980, it looked for a while as if the Jail might be closed by a court order.

Most of the horrors (which as reported sometimes have a whiff of politics about them) seem to have come from administrative troubles, not architectural ones. A citizens' committee in 1970 found the Jail not to be overcrowded, and the general layout of the Jail seems as easy to supervise as any. And yet the media, in reporting events at the Jail, got into the habit of mentioning its age, adjectivally, at the beginnings of their stories. The implication was surely that *if* the Jail worked, it worked in spite of itself.

As an alternative to the old Jail, the citizens of Allegheny County entertained for some ten years the tempting thought of a Hall of Justice, which would house all the County courts and/or jail cells and/or offices. First proposed in 1964, the Hall of Justice died in the state legislature in 1973, in part as a result of lobbying efforts by the Pittsburgh History & Landmarks Foundation; One Oxford Centre has risen where it was to have been. The advocates of the Hall of Justice stressed the desirable unification, the integration of facilities: the courts and the jail under one roof (as, because of the Bridge of Sighs, they had virtually been under Richardson's plan) and the County agencies perhaps in one place instead of being scattered through three official buildings plus rented quarters. An outside consultant submitted a report in 1970 on the County's future space requirements, and these quantified requirements in themselves were surely conducive to the vision of a prismatic mass, rising from the vacant Grant Street site until the ground area was multiplied the requisite number of times to yield the desired square footage.

But what would happen to the Court House and the Jail? What would happen to the City-County Building? Hall of Justice promoters were vague. The Court House—six stories high, a block in area, and subdivided by heavy masonry partitions—"might" become the downtown branch of the Carnegie Library, while the City-County Building "might" become a downtown extension of the University of Pittsburgh. No specific future seems to have been contemplated for the Jail or for the County Office Building, though in 1979 the latter, with a steel frame designed to take additional stories, was suggested as an alternative place for the Jail.

In May of 1973, about the time when agitation for the Hall of Justice was at its height, the Court House and Jail were entered in the National Register of Historic Places. This helped assure the physical preservation of the buildings in two ways: it served notice that they were regarded as of cultural importance to the nation, and it made it almost impossible to use any federal money in a project that would involve their mutilation or demolition. (Later, in July 1976, the Court House and Jail were elevated to the elite category of National Historic Landmarks; fewer than two thousand buildings in the United States enjoy this designation.)

At the request of the Pittsburgh History & Landmarks Foundation, the buildings were also given protection by the City, which designated them "Landmarks." No changes could be made to them without the consent of the City Historic Review Board for six months after notice of a proposal. Since then, the City ordinance has been amended and the six-month provision dropped in order to make decisions by the Board permanent.

The Pittsburgh History & Landmarks Foundation had been following the Hall of Justice campaign with concern. When a KDKA radio and television editorial in February 1972 stigmatized the Court House as "totally inefficient" and referred to the "out-moded, century-old County Jail" as a "monstrosity," Landmarks was quick to reply that, whatever happened, Richardson's buildings should be preserved and carefully modernized. Landmarks suggested that the library branch (which is now in One Mellon Bank Center) could be put in the Jail along with an industrial museum.

Landmarks' concern was not only with the physical preservation of the Court House and Jail but also with their continuation in meaningful public roles. In December 1973 they came forward, in their publication *PH&LF News*, with a detailed proposal based on the County's projected space demands. In brief, they suggested 1) that existing County space in the Court House, City-County Building, and County Office Building be used exclusively for courts and court-related offices; 2) that the Jail continue as the jail; and 3) that office space be created or purchased for other County agencies. This, Landmarks claimed, would save money and use the existing buildings more efficiently. (One argument they made was that the Court House courtrooms could be used more intensively than heretofore.) Unstated, though surely in the minds of Landmarks' officers, was the fitness of having Richardson's two buildings continue in the roles for which they were designed, with the great tower presiding over the center of justice rather than over a warren of miscellaneous offices or civic agencies.

As things turned out, no great changes were made. With the refusal of the Legislature in late 1973 to make funding possible for the Hall of Justice, the Court House, Jail, and other official buildings remained *in statu quo* while the County agencies expanded into rented space where and when it became available.

The great courtyard of the Court House had been praised by Hitchcock in 1936 for its stately arches, its quality as heroic engineering in masonry; but for decades its asphalt pavement had served the humble purpose of a parking lot for County vehicles. Richardson *had* intended it to be entered by vehicles, and had shown it as brick-paved with a horse fountain in the center, but he had surely imagined a more spacious and orderly scene than that which the courtyard presented in the early seventies. A fountain proposal around 1930 came to nothing. In early 1976, though, Katy Flaherty, wife of a County Commissioner, suggested to her husband and to the County's director of planning that the courtyard would be better used as a park. Her idea caught on immediately, at least in some quarters, and the County Department of Planning began exploratory digging on the site in preparation for making plans. One of the three County Commissioners was vehemently opposed to the park and declared that the money spent would be better spent on social services. In September 1976, though, an arrangement was reached whereby the Sarah Scaife Foundation, a Pittsburgh charitable organization, would donate to the Pittsburgh History & Landmarks Foundation the $64,000 needed for materials, while the County would supply the labor. The Commissioners soon voted two-to-one in favor of the park, and two County designers, Samuel Kiss and Carla McDonnell, were assigned to the project along with Ellis L. Schmidlapp, director of historic buildings development with the Pittsburgh History & Landmarks Foundation, which was given the role of design approval. The renovated courtyard (unofficially "Katy's Park") opened May 25, 1977. Almost everyone was pleased.

There were two exceptions, however. The Commissioner who had opposed the park had remained unreconciled, and used to visit the site, while it was being made over, with a conspicuous air of puzzlement. Furthermore, William Huff, once on the architectural faculty at Carnegie-Mellon University and in 1977 at the State University of New York at Buffalo, began an exchange of letters with the officials at Landmarks regarding the quality of the design. He also complained to the Commissioners and in the *Post-Gazette*. The letters to and from Landmarks became quite emotional, but the bases for differing opinion were fairly clear. Huff wanted a rather austere space, empty "at the central point of this spatial theatre, where once a man himself could stand," rather than with the fountain that is actually there: a place from which the handsome courtyard walls could be contemplated without visual distraction. Landmarks, though compromising with the County on some design elements, wanted generally what actually came to be: a refuge from the stir and noise of the city, a place where people could come and rest, talk, eat bag lunches, and enjoy entertainments. Huff, it appeared, thought that the architecture had been betrayed; Landmarks thought that the people had been served and the architectural effects heightened.

As far as the people of Pittsburgh are concerned, Katy's Park has been an unqualified success. In good weather the place is full of people, sitting on the benches, on the dwarf walls of the planter beds, and on the bench around the fountain basin. The fountain plays, now and then the chimes sound from the great tower, and once in a while the space is host to a concert, a play, or a sculpture show. The design could be improved, but the courtyard has come to life, with flowers, trees, and people contrasting their informality with the mass and rigor of Richardson's masonry. In 1979 the State chapter of the American Society of Landscape Architects

"Katy's Park." The former parking lot is now a refuge from the street.

gave Katy Flaherty its annual award for non-professional contribution to landscape architecture.

While the courtyard controversy was going on, late in 1976, preparations were under way to turn Richardson's vaulted entrance hall to the Court House, with its Nesbert murals, into an art gallery. The Courthouse Gallery/Forum had been the idea of Katy Flaherty, once again, and Joan Pierce, wife of another County Commissioner. With Anita Morganstern as director, it opened in December 1976.

The Gallery/Forum gives the public a chance to see changing noncommercial art shows downtown, either in the entrance hall or, in the case of sculpture, in the courtyard. It has been a good thing for the city in that it makes art an accessible weekday affair for masses of working people: no trips to Oakland or Shadyside, no admission fees—just a trip up a flight of stairs in a building halfway along Grant Street. The appeal of such a conception is obvious. On the other hand, the grandeur of Richardson's entrance space, his introductory piece of rhetoric at the foot of his great staircase, is obscured by two zigzag sequences of partitions, and this is undoubtedly unfortunate; Art is quarrelling with Architecture (even though architecture *is* an art), and some day the quarrel should be resolved with the provision of an equally useful, equally accessible, but less sensitive space for the Gallery/Forum.

One of the Gallery/Forum's early shows, opened in September 1977, concerned the Court House and Jail themselves. Maintenance people in County employ had retained the working drawings, ink on linen, that Richardson's office had turned out in the mid-'80s; these, however, had been regarded by the few who were aware of them as utilitarian affairs, and no one had thought of studying or displaying them. It was not generally known, besides, that many of the drawings for the 1883 competition, by Richardson, Myers, Boyington, and Ord, were still in a vault in the Court House attic. In late 1976 and early 1977, though, the County Department of Parks, which was responsible for the Courthouse Gallery/Forum, began to study the drawings seriously and realized what a treasure the County had kept, more or less unconsciously, for over 90 years.

The handsome show of 24 presentation drawings and linens was, like the Chicago Tribune competition of 1922, a revealing look at the state of the architectural art, as applied to a certain design problem, in a certain year. Franklin B. Toker, of the Department of Architecture at Carnegie-Mellon University, wrote a paper, "Richardson 'en concours,' " that appeared in the November 1977 *Carnegie Magazine*, in which he compared the designs and pointed out the lucidity of Richardson's original conception, its ability to take the Commissioners' complicated specifications of 1883 and translate them into a deceptively simple-looking plan and an exterior that accords with the plan. Toker's paper gave a convincing account of the rationale of Richardson's general design, and showed that the County had chosen the best design by far of those submitted. His argument was debatable mostly in its statement that Richardson regarded the great tower as "meaningless symbolism." The tower somehow has never been quite respectable in a century overshadowed with utilitarianism. It has never really *done* very much; it has, primarily, been a symbol. It has been under the stigma of being useless, except as art is useful. In the early '70s for instance, trees began to appear, conspicuously, between its capstones, and it was several years before they were removed. They were unsightly and their roots might have pried the stones apart, but there were other demands on County funds that seemed more pressing. And yet, any implication that Richardson was less than enthusiastic about the tower seems refuted by the sheer quality of its design.

Finally, in September 1980, the County Controller, going through old files, discovered a box of documents having to do with the early days of the present Court House. These included: the agreement with Richardson, in 1883, to supply plans, elevations, sections, a perspective, skeleton specifications, and an estimate for his competition design in return for $2,500 (he was given two months); the formal approval of Richardson's design, dated July 3, 1884; the letter from Thomas Mellon warning the Commissioners, *in re* W. H. Brown vs. County Commissioners, not to spend any money on the Richardson plan; contracts and receipts; a letter from Richardson about design of the furniture, protesting that it was too early to start and that the users of the spaces should have a say on what was wanted; and finally the specifications, a lengthy document in which the whole building was anatomized. (It is interesting to note that the roof, actually red tile under all the dirt, was at first to be of slate, and that the grand stair and its surroundings were to be finished in brown or red sandstone, not the Bedford limestone that was actually used.)

Early in the 1980s, two office towers rose near the Court House, far overtopping it yet each, in its own way, designed in an attempt not to overwhelm it. One Oxford Center, by Hellmuth, Obata and Kassabaum of New York, has chamfers and reentering angles intended to break up an otherwise hulking mass, to create the fiction of four slender octagonal shafts in a cluster. One Mellon Bank Center, by Welton Becket Associates' New York office, stands much closer, just across Fifth Avenue from the Court House; it attempts even greater harmony with strong verticals around an octagonal shaft, mansard roof-like terminations to its masses, and a grey finish to its metal walls not too different from the color of the Court House granite. The latter building's ground plan, furthermore, is skewed toward Fifth Avenue to open an oblique view of the side wall of the Court House.

Pressure on the Jail, limited by a recent court order to 510 prisoners, was alleviated by the opening, in 1986, of an annex close by. This, an adaptation of the 1920-period Jones Law Building combined with extensive new construction, had a capacity of 280. Early in 1987 there was talk of enlarging the annex still further. At the same time, the County was planning a study of Richardson's Jail and its future.

The year 1988 was the bicentennial of Allegheny County and its Court of Common Pleas, and the centennial of the Court House. The occasion was marked in several ways. A series of events, sponsored by the Bicentennial Commission of Allegheny County, climaxed in a parade on September 24, the anniversary. The Commission and the Pittsburgh History & Landmarks Foundation released this book on the same date. Its writing was paid for by a grant from the Edgar Kaufmann Charitable Foundation, and assistance toward its publication, among other sources, included a grant from the 1988 Bicentennial Committee of the Court of Common Pleas and graphic art services supplied by the County.

In recognition of the Court House centennial, the chairman of the Bicentennial Commission, James W. Knox, appointed the Allegheny County Courthouse Restoration Committee in 1987, a 19-member group headed by Arthur P. Ziegler, Jr., president of Landmarks. Its purpose was manifold: to advise on repairs to the building, a particular cause of concern being the deteriorated roof of shingle tile; to undo the haphazard remodelings and additions of a century; to advise on future space utilization, construction, furnishing, and graphics; and to comment on studies in progress on the future of the Jail. A lead grant from the National Trust for Historic Preservation gave the Committee's work a particular advantage by paying for the services of two restoration architects from Landmarks Design Associates to advise on future improvements for a limited period. It hoped that the availability of this knowledgeable advice would prompt the County to seek such advice in the future, as a matter of course, whenever alterations were planned.

The Restoration Committee's expectations could not go beyond protection of major architectural elements and the accommodation of modern uses in a coherent, well-integrated interior, but the Court House's centennial year saw something close to a full restoration of one courtroom. Room 321, the original Small Orphan's Court, became the subject of a project sponsored by the Fund for the Bicentennial Celebration of the Court of Common Pleas. In the course of the work, for which UDA Architects were the designers, two dropped ceilings were removed to reveal the full 27-foot height beneath a ceiling of brick vaults and iron joists resting on a mighty iron box girder; modern utility systems were invisibly installed; woodwork was refinished and decorative work was reinstalled or reproduced; and the whole room above the oaken wainscotting was painted, the wall color being sage green. The before-and-after contrast was most dramatic, a living example for the Restoration Committee to use in showing how the grandeur of a public building can be nibbled at by years of relaxed standards and little expediencies.

Right: Room 321, mid-1980s.

Opposite: Room 321 after restoration.

In 1890, the tower of the Court House dominated Pittsburgh with the same assured ease that smaller court houses, purposefully sited on Western Pennsylvania hilltops, dominate their rural county seats. Its masonry, still clean-looking in old photographs, reigned serenely over the smoky industrial improvisations, the cast-iron store fronts, the Italianate office-building facades, the spindly spires, and the little houses of the unruly mid-Victorian city. This was not to last. A decade after its debut in Chicago, the skeleton building frame had come to Pittsburgh and the downtown skyline began to heave upward. Now there are steel towers, very big ones, close by, and the Court House tower is hidden from a good many distant viewpoints. Yet it has not lost dignity. The building as a whole seems dwarfed by the new constructions; its romantic roofs and dormers seem archaic against the sheer, bland surfaces of business architecture. The tower, though, is too inherently good a work of art to be downed or humiliated by mere mass and height. It will always look serene, and indeed tall, whatever rises around and above it.

UNION T
Guaranty Co

A last look at Richardson's drafting room. To the draftsman's left is the competition perspective of the County Buildings, with a Jail elevation above.

EPILOGUE

James D. Van Trump

The saga of a great building is essentially a grand human artifact, a flowering and the symbol of the age and the culture that produced it. The American court house is profoundly a part of the American experience, both as an institution and as a material structure. Pittsburgh's first Court House in Market Square, and then the monumental Greek Revival Court House on Grant's Hill, were part of a pattern that evolved throughout the expanding nation. The late 19th and early 20th centuries carried this evolution further, with larger and more complex buildings in a variety of styles. During this period, Allegheny County was different only that it happened to secure a work of architectural genius—Richardson's Allegheny County Court House and Jail.

This last great work of Henry Hobson Richardson is now sure of preservation since its inclusion in the National Register of Historic Places, and also since it has been placed among the National Historic Landmarks. The general public, through the constant efforts of the Pittsburgh History & Landmarks Foundation and other partisans of preservation, is now better informed as to the architectural significance of the Richardson Court House and Jail. Modern court houses—since the institution still seems to be secure—are being built, but Pittsburgh's own monument will not have to give way to new trends. Indeed, the Allegheny County Court House and Jail are a national treasure.

But what now, what of the future? A great building truly lives only as it is informed with the life about it. Since the opening of the Richardson Court House in 1888 there have been a number of exterior and interior changes, and the context of the structure has changed almost out of recognition. Further minor structural changes may occur, new proposals and projects will surely continue to be discussed in connection with these great buildings, and the city itself will be ever-changing. Vigilance will be required, as it has been in the past, to see that these unavoidable changes are kept within bounds.

I myself, when I want to see the Court House in its total context, go to Mt. Washington—and surely one of the great urban views of America unfolds before me. There, in the midst of the sky-reaching corporate headquarters buildings, rises the Court House tower. It still raises its rugged head and continues to stand as a symbol of our city.

An epilogue, like the *envoi* of a poem, should be brief. As one looks down on the city where Richardson's tower still reigns secure, one is sure that as long as Pittsburgh endures, so will the Court House.

BIBLIOGRAPHY

"Allegheny County Court-house, The." *Harper's Weekly,* 32:16 (October 6, 1888), 751.

Baldwin, Leland D., *Pittsburgh: The Story of a City.* Pittsburgh: University of Pittsburgh Press, 1937

Brackenridge, Henry Marie, *Recollections of Persons and Places in the West.* Pittsburgh: John I. Kay, 1834.

"County Buildings at Pittsburgh, The." *Harper's Weekly,* 29:1471 (February 29, 1885), 142.

Hetherington, Edwin, S., "The Allegheny Courthouse and Jail by Henry Hobson Richardson." Thesis, Dept. of Art and Archaeology, Princeton University, 1971.

Hitchcock, Henry Russell, Jr., *The Architecture of H. H. Richardson and His Times.* New York: Museum of Modern Art, 1936.

Huff, William S., "Richardson's Jail." *Western Pennsylvania Historical Magazine,* 41:1 (Spring, 1958), 41-59.

Kilkelly, Sarah, H., *The Story of Pittsburgh: Its Rise and Progress.* Pittsburgh: B. C. & Gordon Montgomery Co., 1906.

McKee, Charles H., *History of the Erection of the Court House.* [no other data available].

Mumford, Lewis, *The Brown Decades: A Study of the Arts in America, 1865-1895.* New York: Harcourt, Brace & Co., 1931.

——— *Sticks and Stones: A Study of American Arts and Civilization.* New York: Boni and Liveright, Inc., 1924.

Ochsner, Jeffrey Karl, *H. H. Richardson: Complete Architectural Works.* Cambridge, Mass.: MIT Press, 1982.

Official Report of the Dedicatory Exercises Held at the New Court House at the City of Pittsburgh, County of Allegheny, on Monday, September 24, A.D. 1888. Pittsburgh: William G. Johnston & Co., 1888.

O'Gorman, James F., *H. H. Richardson and His Office.* Cambridge, Mass.: Harvard College Library, 1974.

Proposed Changes to Court House: Report of Committee Appointed to Investigate the Advisability of Same. Pittsburgh: Allegheny County Bar Association, 1904.

Richardson, Henry Hobson, *County Buildings for Allegheny, Pa.: Specification for Court House.* [No other data available].

——*Description of Drawings for the Proposed New County Buildings for Allegheny County, Penn.* Boston: Printed for private circulation, 1884.

Schuyler, Montgomery, "The Building of Pittsburgh." *Architectural Record,* (September, 1911), 203-82.

Stotz, Charles Morse, *The Early Architecture of Western Pennsylvania.* New York: William Helburn, Inc., for the Buhl Foundation, 1936.

Thurston, George H., *Allegheny County's Hundred Years.* Pittsburgh: A. H. Anderson & Son, 1888.

Van Rensselaer, Marianna Griswold, *Henry Hobson Richardson and His Works.* Boston and New York: Houghton, Mifflin & Co., 1888.

Van Trump, James D., "The Church Beyond Fashion." *Charette,* 38:4 (April, 1958), 26-29.

——"The Romanesque Revival in Pittsburgh." *Journal of the Society of Architectural Historians,* 16:3 (October, 1957), 22-29.

INDEX

Alden, Frank, supervising architect, 84
Alden & Harlow, architects, 142,147,148
Allegheny (city), 2
Allegheny Cemetery, 17-18
Allegheny County, Pennsylvania
—bicentennial observances, 167, 169
—formed, 1-2
—progress, 1788-1888, 93
Allegheny County Mortuary, 130, 131
American Institute of Architects,
Pittsburgh Chapter, 150-52
Austin, Charles D., supervising architect, 84
Bicentennial Commission of Allegheny County, 167
Bigelow, Edward Manning, City Engineer, 84, 138
Boyington, William W., architect, 38, 50, 52, 63
Brackenridge, Henry Marie, author, 12-13
Brackenridge, Hugh Henry, lawyer and author, 11-12
Braddock, Gen. Edward, 11
Bridge of Sighs, 90, 91, 105, 109, 120
Buffalo: City and County Hall, 33, 34
Burke's Building, 17, 24
Campbell, Col. John, 2-3
Chislett, John, architect, 17-18
City-County Building, 24-25, 143, 144-47
County Office Building, 130, 154-55
Court House (first), 1-9
—circuit courts, 6-7
—completion, 2, 3, 5
—demolition, 8
—deterioration, 8
—evidence regarding, 3
—exterior, 3-4
—interior, 4-5
—jail, 7
—precedents, 5
—theatricals, 6
—uses, 6
Court House (second) 16-26, 29-30, 32
—burned, 29-30
—construction begun, 19
—designed, 19
—deterioration, 25-26
—exterior, 19-20
—interior and plan, 20, 23
—jail, 23, 35

—occupation, 19
—reconstruction proposed, 32
—site acquired, 13
—stylistic mixture, 20
Court House (present)
—adjacent modern buildings, 167
—alterations to entrances, 147-48
—alterations to interior, 156, 160, 165-66, 169
—alterations to surroundings, 142
—Bridge of Sighs, 90
—carillon, 160
—Commissioners' requirements, 36, 42
—competition designs, 50-59
—competition drawings discovered, 166
—construction, 70, 76-79, 83
—contractors, 67-68
—cornerstone laid, 74-75
—courtyard, 163-65
—criticism and analysis, 71-72, 73, 97, 104-10, 114, 116-25, 166
—dedication, 92-95
—design competition, 36-37
—design modifications, 63, 65
—documents discovered, 166-67
—electric lighting, 85
—enlargement proposed, 128, 130, 132, 134-38, 139, 140, 148, 150
—furniture, 79, 85, 88
—Gallery/Forum, 165-66
—imitations, 116
—joinery, 80, 86
—law library, 89
—lion sculptures, 85-87
—materials, 34, 36, 78-79
—National Historic Landmark, 171
—object of pride, 93-94, 95
—proposed, 32
—proposed as City Hall, 138
—protests and legal action against, 68, 69, 70
—Restoration Committee, 167-68
—restoration of Room 321, 168
—Richardson competition designs and specifications, 50, 54-59, 60
—Richardson competition plan praised, 59
—stonecutting, 81, 83, 86
—structure completed, 85, 88
—tower, 63, 65, 127, 170
Davis, Charles, County Engineer, 33, 34, 35
Diamond, the (Market Square), 1, 2-3
Diamond Street (Forbes Avenue), 20
Emmanuel Episcopal Church, Allegheny (North Side), 40, 41, 42
Evans and Tombs, stonecutters, 81, 119
Flaherty, Katy, 164, 165
First Baptist Church, 29
Forbes, Gen. John, 11
Forbes, Avenue (Diamond Street), 20
Fort Duquesne, 11

Frick Building, 24, 27, 128
Gibbs, D. W., and Company, architects, 74
Gibson, Mrs. E. F., sketch of Pittsburgh, 1
Grant, Maj. James, 11
Grant's Hill, 10-15, 28
—construction on, 14, 27-28
Greek Revival in Pittsburgh, 18-19
—echoed in later buildings, 24-25
Hamilton, Ohio: Butler County Courthouse competition, 74
Hornbostel, Henry, architect, 139, 140, 144
Huff, William, professor of architecture, 164
"Hump," the, 14-15, 16, 20, 21, 27, 84, 132, 139, 142
Jail (present)
—annex built, 167
—Bridge of Sighs, 90, 91
—completion, 77, 81, 83, 85
—construction, 76
—criticism and analysis, 104-06, 114, 116, 120-23, 124
—enlargement, 128, 130-32
—proposed, 32, 35
—reputation, 161-62
—threatened, 150-52, 154, 156, 158-60
Landmarks Design Associates, architects, 169
Lee, Edward B., architect, 145
Loughy, Dennis, poet, 7
Marie, John, tavern keeper, 13
Market Square, (the Diamond), 1, 2-3, 13
military training, 28
Myers, Elijah, architect, 38, 40, 50, 51, 74
Nesbert, Vincent, artist, 156
Norcross Brothers, contractors, 68, 69, 78, 88
Ord, John, architect, 37, 38, 50, 53
Oregon House, tavern, 28
Osterling, Frederick John, architect, 130, 131, 132
Palmer, Hornbostel & Jones, architects, 145
Peebles, Andrew, architect, 37, 38, 39, 49
Penn family, 2
Pittsburgh
—in 1817, 1
—growth, 13-14
—and Greek Revival, 18-19
Pittsburgh History & Landmarks Foundation, 163, 164, 167
Post, George B., architect, 37
public square beside Court House proposed, 138
Richardson, Henry Hobson
—active on County Buildings working drawings, 63
—at time of County Buildings competition, 40
—impact of death, 81, 83
—in County Buildings competition, 42, 44, 54-59
—life and work, 44, 46, 48
—memorialized at Court House, 88-89
—selected as County Buildings architect, 59
Robitser, T. P., artist, 8
Roush, Stanley Lawson, County Architect, 148, 149, 151, 154, 155

Rutan, Russell & Wood, architects, 150
St. Paul's R. C. Church (Cathedral), 27
St. Peter's Episcopal Church, Pittsburgh, 27-28
Sarah Scaife Foundation, 164
Shepley, Rutan and Coolidge, architects, 79-80, 81, 83-84, 85, 88, 119
Solon, archon, 19
Trimble, Maurice, architect, 139
Tucker, John D., artist, 4, 8
UDA Architects, architects, 169
University of Pittsburgh (Western University of Pennsylvania), 28-29
Vickroy, Thomas, surveyor, 2
Weber, Edward J., architect, 152, 154
Western University of Pennsylvania (University of Pittsburgh), 28-29, 31
Wood, Eric Fisher, architect, 148
Woods, George, surveyor, 2

This book was typeset by the Allegheny County Graphics Department in Palacio, and was printed on Vintage Velvet text by Hoechstetter Printing Co. Cover and book design by Thomas S. Stevenson, Jr., of Landmarks Design Associates, with the assistance of Denise Duncan of the Allegheny County Graphics Department.